Side by Side

SIDE BY SIDE

Alice and Staughton Lynd, the Ohio Years

Mark W. Weber

Stephen H. Paschen

THE KENT STATE UNIVERSITY PRESS

KENT, OHIO

This publication is made possible in part by the generous
support of the following individuals:

Felisa L. Anthony

Matthew Berlin

Susan T. Berlin

G. G. W. Hays

Lynn Salzbrenner

Jeanne and John J. Somers

Merle Stern

Shari Turitz

This book is dedicated to the following fallen comrades:

Edward Mann

John Barbero

Stan Weir

Martin Glaberman

Lessley Harmon

The ideals for which they struggled will be with us always.

Friendship is born at that moment when one person says to another: "What you too? I thought I was the only one."

C. S. Lewis

CONTENTS

FOREWORD

Alice Lynd once observed that "there is something about . . . political convictions or a sense that 'this is what has to be done' which gives strength." She reminds us that "the example of another person may help" us to gain that strength to resist illegitimate authority. Mark Weber and Stephen Paschen chart the lives of two such powerful exemplars of lives committed to containing arbitrary power and injustice: Alice and Staughton Lynd. This work traces the Lynds' struggles to assist draft resisters in the early 1970s and steelworkers in the legendary and tragic labor disputes in Youngstown, as well as chronicling their unflinching commitment to death row inmates at the Southern Ohio Correctional Facility.

Weber and Paschen's fine book complements and extends my efforts in *The Admirable Radical: Staughton Lynd and Cold War Dissent, 1945–1970*. They pick up the tale in the 1970s, where I left off, as my principal concerns were the social movements of the 1960s and Staughton's pivotal role in some of those movements. My biography of Lynd, this book on the Ohio years, and Andrej Grubacic's *From Here to There: The Staughton Lynd Reader* constitute a sort of nonfiction trilogy that, taken together, offer a complete narrative of the Lynds' five decades of activism and writing.

I first decided to write about Lynd after we worked together in the middle of the first decade of the 2000s to organize a series of panels on military resistance from World War II to Operation Iraqi Freedom. We assembled a panel of veterans who had developed antiwar views either as a result of their military service or for a variety of personal reasons. These panels demonstrated to me the power of oral history testimony in a time of crisis. Vietnam veterans spoke of the fabricated Gulf of Tonkin incident of August 1964 that propelled the United States into a senseless war—a war that, much later, even Robert McNamara, at the time the U.S. secretary of defense, would admit was "wrong." Veterans

of Iraq Operation Freedom questioned the validity of the Bush administration's claims that the Iraqi regime possessed weapons of mass destruction. During these times of crises, what are now discredited as outright
lies were treated as serious contested topics that required "objective"
analysis and debate. The attack at Tonkin never occurred and Iraq did
not have weapons of mass destruction, yet a frightened public was de-
ceived into supporting imperial ambitions. The veteran panels provided
an antidote to mainstream narratives. The antiwar veterans seemed to
see through the fog of deception before many scholars and public com-
mentators. Lynd, through practice and example rather than preaching
and lecturing, showed me the usefulness of oral history. I went on to
publish a book of soldier testimony about the Iraq war. Lynd remembers
the legendary historian Howard Zinn sitting in his Atlanta apartment in
the 1960s recording members of the Student Nonviolent Coordinating
Committee (SNCC) discussing their courageous work in the civil rights
movement. Zinn had taught Lynd that oral history was a powerful
weapon against prevailing narratives; later, Lynd taught me the same.

The Lynds' activist lives—from their civil rights work to their present-day commitment to death row inmates—also provide a compelling antidote to orthodox narratives. In the 1960s, social activists gave
priority to "organizing" others into a social justice program. Many of
these efforts were noble and worthwhile, but Staughton has come to see
organizing in a much different light, what he calls "accompaniment."
Weber and Paschen's book is especially useful as a "set of reflections on
accompaniment," as experienced by Staughton and Alice during their
years in Ohio. It illustrates how accompaniment is the outgrowth of
Alice and Staughton Lynd's lifelong commitment to social justice. A
key component of accompaniment is for the so-called organizer to lend
his or her expertise to a community in struggle, while at the time recognizing that the community members are the experts on their experience and conditions. Such recognition ensures that the ordinary people
guide and shape the decision-making process, rather than the organizer
arriving in a community as an outsider with a preconceived set of ideas
on what should be done. In short, "the radical substitutes a specific set
of skills in place of ideology," and "actually live[s] in the community
among the poor" as they accompany each other on the road to long-
term commitment to change.

Staughton takes the term *accompaniment* from Oscar Romero, the Salvadoran archbishop, who was assassinated while delivering mass in 1980. In 1993, a United Nations truth commission named former Major Roberto d'Aubuisson, a leader of El Salvador's far right, as the mastermind behind this cold-hearted assassination; a former National Guard officer, d'Aubuisson had been trained at the U.S. Army facility in Georgia. Also according to UN reports, assassins from the death squads d'Aubuisson formed and controlled, who killed Jesuit priests in a separate incident, were likewise connected to the same U.S. Army training center.

Without equating the two, both Oscar Romero and Staughton Lynd have been targets of considerable criticism for taking "radical" stances against U.S. policies. No rational person would side with those who killed priests in Latin America during the 1980s. But who today could argue that the Lynds' stance on civil rights or the Vietnam War was misguided? Should they have remained quiet as white segregationists hung black folks from trees? One thing that inspired me to write a biography of Staughton Lynd was his participation in the civil rights movement, especially his service as coordinator of the Mississippi Freedom Schools. These schools were part of the broader Mississippi Freedom Summer campaign, where black and white volunteers worked in solidarity to dismantle segregation through voter registration, Freedom Schools, community centers, and special projects. When white segregationists murdered three of these volunteers—Michael Schwerner, James Chaney, and Andrew Goodman—Staughton responded with determination. In a violent army, when your comrade is killed, he argued, you pick up his rifle and shoot back. In a nonviolent army, you pick up that person's dream and make it a reality.

The Lynds have been working to make justice and equality a reality for more than five decades. In an age of illegal government surveillance, drone strikes, and perpetual war, when wages stagnate or decline as corporate and CEO profits soar, there is indeed something about the political convictions of the Lynds that gives us strength to fight for a better world.

CARL MIRRA
2013

INTRODUCTION AND
ACKNOWLEDGMENTS

> He allowed himself to be swayed by his conviction that
> human beings are not born once and for all on the day
> their mothers gave birth to them, but that life obliges
> them over and over to give birth to themselves.
>
> GABRIEL GARCIA MARQUEZ, *Love in the Time of Cholera*

This book is about two people and an idea. The idea did not originate with them and it does not end with them. The idea is called *accompaniment* and the two people are Alice and Staughton Lynd. By practicing this idea in the real life struggles of working people, these two people have changed the lives of many, including their own.

On 12 June 1976, Alice and Staughton celebrated their twenty-fifth wedding anniversary with a renewal of their wedding vows. The celebration was held in Chicago, where the Lynds had been living for several years. Just two months later, however, Alice and Staughton would leave friends in Chicago to begin a new life in Youngstown, Ohio, a mill city near the border with Pennsylvania. Thirty-five years later, in the spring of 2011, Alice and Staughton celebrated their sixtieth wedding anniversary at the Catholic Worker house in Youngstown. The story that unfolded between these two anniversary celebrations is the general subject of this book. When the couple left Chicago, they were in their mid-forties. By the time of the celebration at the Catholic Worker house, they were in their early eighties.

Staughton first met Alice Niles in Cambridge, Massachusetts, in 1950, when he was twenty-one and she was twenty years old. Staughton

was studying for his B.A. at Harvard at the time, while Alice was studying at Radcliffe. Introduced by Staughton's roommate, they found much
in common, both in background and in their interests. Staughton Lynd
was born in 1929 to famous sociologists Helen and Robert Lynd, authors of *Middletown*, the study of class inequality in Muncie, Indiana,
and was initially educated at Fieldston School, run by the New York
Society for Ethical Culture. Alice was also born to parents concerned
with social and political issues. Both her father, Henry Edward Niles,
and her mother, Mary-Cushing Howard, were college graduates involved in social activism. Concerned, according to Alice, with issues of
"world peace, gender, and race,"[1] they had both become Quakers in the
1940s. By the time he met Alice, Staughton was already a socialist, and
was impressed when she remarked that she had read *The Decline and
Fall of British Capitalism*.

The couple married in 1951 and began a life together that included
peace activism, civil rights activity, and community organizing. From
1954 to 1957, they were members of the Macedonia Cooperative Community in Clarksville, Georgia. By 1960 Staughton was completing a
Ph.D. in history at Columbia University, and in 1961 he accepted a
position teaching history at Spelman College in Atlanta, a prestigious
college for African American women. In 1963, his political activism
prompted the Student Nonviolent Coordinating Committee (SNCC) to
invite Staughten to direct the Freedom Schools that were a part of the
1964 Mississippi Summer Project. In 1965, Staughton, together with
Tom Hayden, leader of the Students for a Democratic Society (SDS),
and Marxist historian Herbert Aptheker, visited North Vietnam. He
chaired the first march against the Vietnam War and later, after moving
to Chicago, graduated from law school at the University of Chicago.
Staughton is a prolific writer and author of many books.

Alice has training in early childhood education. She has directed
daycare centers and worked as a draft counselor during the period of
the Vietnam War. Alice became a paralegal and in 1985 received her
law degree from the University of Pittsburgh. Between 1985 and 1990,
the Lynds visited Nicaragua together several times and later traveled
to Israel and the Occupied Territories. The Lynds also worked together
to edit *Rank and File: Personal Histories of Rank and File Organizers*,
Homeland, and *Nonviolence in America: A Documentary History*.

Together Alice and Staughton practiced law at Northeast Ohio Legal Services until their retirement in 1996.

Alice and Staughton have three children. When they moved to Ohio in 1976, Barbara was almost twenty-one and Lee was eighteen and heading off to college. Only little Martha, nine years old, would be living at home on Timbers Court in Niles, Ohio, near Youngstown. As we write this manuscript, Barbara Lynd Bond, fifty-seven, is a kindergarten teacher in a Catholic school in the Youngstown area. Lee Lynd, now fifty-three, is a senior professor at Dartmouth University's Thayer School of Engineering. He is an expert on bioenergy. Martha Lynd married Horacio Enrique (Kique) Altan and makes her home in San Marcos, Guatemala, where she is a masseuse and assists Guatemalan women, widowed in *"la violencia"* in the 1980s, to sell their weavings in markets outside the country.

The practice of accompaniment by both Alice and Staughton in the years following their 1976 move to Youngstown from Chicago was a conscious decision on their part, made at a time when both were middle-aged and had been activists for more than twenty years. There is no doubt that Staughton's adoption of accompaniment was fueled in part by his experience in the early New Left; its values of local organizing, decentralized decision-making, and living with the people helped prepare him for his later adoption of accompaniment as a lens through which to see a different kind of social change. Staughton may also have been prompted by his revulsion against the hierarchical culture of the Old Left, at its heyday in the 1930s and early 1940s; frustration with this culture, which emphasized party discipline and political programs and featured frequent splits and expulsions, led Staughton and his young comrades of the 1960s to search for viable alternatives. In contrast, New Left politics (to the extent that it is wise to generalize) featured consensus, long discussions, and practical action over theory. As for Alice, her adoption of accompaniment came through her work in draft counseling, which required listening to each young man seeking help and acknowledging that he is the expert on his own life. The Lynds' decision to employ accompaniment as a new tool for social change came during a time when several of the movements in which Alice and Staughton had placed hope seemed to be transmogrifying into their opposites.

Two examples of this shift occurred in the latter half of the 1960s. The first was the move in 1968 by the SDS to embrace Leninism, Maoism, and other Old Left values—the very values that the New Left had originally set out to challenge or at least avoid. The second was the SNCC's gradual movement after 1965 away from its commitment to nonviolence and toward integration into revolutionary black nationalism, with the result that whites in the organization were asked to leave.

Other factors making the Lynds temperamentally suited to practice accompaniment were their experience with Quaker practices, Alice's draft counselor listening skills, and Staughton's preference as a radical historian for listening to the experiences of ordinary people. The essence of accompaniment is the commitment by the radical to move to a community of poor or working people in order to place his or her skills (whether in law, medicine, clergy, or teaching) in the service of ordinary people struggling to survive. The young radical choosing to accompany the poor or workers in struggle understands that he or she is not going to preach to the people about politics or a particular party or candidate. Instead, the radical simply offers skills to the people and walks with them in their struggles.

The Lynds have found inspiration for accompaniment from their own experiences and from the experiences and wisdom of others. One of the most profound influences on Alice and Staughton has been the accompaniment vision offered by the late Archbishop Oscar Romero of El Salvador. Romero, who was murdered in 1980, effectively expressed his thoughts and feelings in four pastoral letters.[2] Other than Catholic priests and nuns living in poor communities in Latin America, it is difficult to find people (especially radicals) who have chosen to live in a community of poor or working class families and work with them on their day-to-day struggles. The Lynds are two such radicals and it is their story that we seek to tell.

Perhaps we should offer a word or two about the two of us. Steve Paschen is a writer, historian, and archivist who has written several books on Ohio and American history. A skilled and perceptive interviewer, he helped to organize the interviews with Alice and Staughton as well as those with friends and associates of the Lynds. Mark Weber is the retired dean of libraries at Kent State University. As an undergraduate in the early 1960s, he was associated with various organizations and political currents on the American left that would shape his perspective for more than fifty years.

The authors wish to thank the following individuals, who read all or portions of the manuscript and who offered constructive criticism: Carl Mirra, Greg Wilson, Alice Lynd, Staughton Lynd, Linda Silver, and the staff of The Kent State University Press. We would also like to thank Lae'l Hughes-Watkins and Liz Traina, interested young researchers who performed supportive research and transcribed some of the interviews. Finally, we would like to thank the staffs of the State Historical Society of Wisconsin and the Department of Special Collections and Archives at Kent State University for their assistance.

It is also important for us to thank the following individuals, who agreed to be interviewed as part of this research project. In the years since their move to Youngstown in 1976, Alice and Staughton have "accompanied" each of the people interviewed (and many more) in their struggles. Except for the multiple interviews we conducted with Alice and Staughton Lynd, they are listed below in the order in which we interviewed them.

Alice and Staughton Lynd: 9 November 2009; 15 January, 16 March, 18 March, 20 April, and 18 May 2010; 15 January, 20 January, and 16 December 2011; 6 January and 16 March 2012; and 14 January and 9 September 2013.

Charles McCollester: 11 November 2010

Mike Stout: 11 November 2010

Tony Budak: 14 January 2011

Ed Wells: 8 April 2011

Beth Hepfner: 25 April 2011

Jim Jordan: 29 July 2011

John Sharick: 15 August 2011

Theresa Lyons: 4 November 2011

Gail Phares: 20 January 2012

Keith LaMar: 18 September and 25 October 2012

Jason Robb: 25 September and 11 November 2012

Martha Lynd Altan: 14 July 2013

Alexis Buss: 11 August 2013 (by telephone)

James Callen: 15 August 2013

Eric O'Neill: 23 August 2013
Lorry Swain: 23 August 2013
Jules Lobel: 11 September 2013

The interviews listed above were conducted using the standard methodology for oral history interviews, with the following exceptions. The interviews with Jason Robb and Keith LaMar were conducted inside the Ohio State Prison in Youngstown, where the two men are on death row for their alleged part in the Lucasville prison uprising of April 1993; visitors are not permitted to bring books, notebooks, pencils, or recording devices into the prison. The interview with Gail Phares, peace activist with and one of the founders of Witness for Peace, took place during a long bus ride on the back roads of Colombia going from Cali to Buenaventura.

Of course, a special thanks must go to Alice and Staughton, who read the manuscript, corrected our mistakes, and offered their own observations on our interpretation of people and events. At no time did they attempt to control the perspectives we offered in the book.

While both of us were familiar with the writings of Alice and Staughton before beginning this project, we each came to know of the Lynds in different ways. Steve knew the Lynds from Staughton's books and through his knowledge of the Alice and Staughton Lynd Papers in the Department of Special Collections and Archives at Kent State University. He first met the Lynds in the fall of 2009 when we were contemplating embarking on this project. He marveled that Staughton had so many stories to tell from his experiences of sixty years of activism. He also noted that Alice was a very careful listener who "didn't miss a thing." Mark heard Staughton speak at the University of Wisconsin in the fall of 1970 and then later in Cleveland in 1986. He became personally acquainted with the Lynds in April 1998, when Staughton was invited by the Kent State University Library to speak at the Friends of the Library Dinner. Mark has since collaborated with the Lynds on several projects and kept in touch with them over the years.

Others have written about the Lynds. Carl Mirra, for example, published a fine scholarly biography of Staughton's activities from 1945 to 1970.[3] Our book differs from these other books in two ways. First, it is a study of both Alice and Staughton Lynd. Second, it is a thematic reflection by the two of us on the life of the Lynds in Ohio, as seen through the lens of accompaniment, rather than a comprehensive scholarly biography of the Lynds since they moved to Ohio in 1976.

Following the high-profile mass actions of the 1960s, many activists moved on to careers in academia, jobs with labor unions, or work in Democratic Party politics or in the many social justice organizations that came out of the 1960s. As professors, state senators, union officials, or policy analysts, these figures addressed the issue of justice at a macro level but rarely worked directly with ordinary workers and their families. Alice and Staughton made a conscious decision to move to a largely working-class community and to "accompany" workers and their families—rank-and-file activists, retirees, prisoners, and the poor—in their daily struggles.

The Lynds have worked together as partners and share many basic values. However, there are some basic differences in Staughton's and Alice's frames of reference. Staughton has written much more about the struggles they have shared than has Alice. Both have played important roles but usually the analysis and description is expressed through Staughton's voice. While they share a common grounding in the teachings and values of the Quaker religion, Staughton's political and intellectual connections are with the political and religious left.

Alice's work is grounded in her ability to foster interpersonal relationships with the people she assists. Staughton's contributions to a given project often involve a theoretical analysis that reflects both his extensive reading and a lifetime of carefully observed experience. Alice's experience is likewise an important asset, together with her keen investigatory sense, meticulous attention to detail, identification of relevant facts, ability to determine objective applicable criteria, and presentation of a case or topic so as to depict it as both distinctive and compelling. She prefers to do the task at hand rather than write about the past.

It is not surprising that two such people have spent a lifetime together struggling to create a better world and searching for a sense of community. Our interviews with the Lynds revealed not only a partnership of strength, action, and intellectual ability, but also a gentle, mutual respect for each other and for their fellow humans. It is these qualities that have impelled them to reach out to workers, the elderly, and prisoners, even when these people hold political views that are diametrically opposed to their own.

Chapter One ～◯

BURNHAM'S DILEMMA

"It took me years to solve Burnham's dilemma."

STAUGHTON LYND

The Vanguard Party

On 22 March 2012, one of the authors traveled with Alice and Staughton Lynd to a labor educator's conference in Pittsburgh. In the car, the author told Staughton that he thought Staughton's efforts to solve the dilemma posed by James Burnham in his 1940 book, *The Managerial Revolution*, were the key to understanding his attraction to participatory democracy in the 1960s and 1970s and later, after the move to Ohio, his belief in accompaniment. Staughton responded: "Yes, there you have it." Riding in the back seat, Alice responded: "Yes, but that does not explain my belief in accompaniment." Not surprisingly, two lifelong companions in various struggles took the same journey but followed different paths. In this chapter, we will deal with Staughton's journey to accompaniment, addressing the somewhat different journey that Alice made in the next.

In his book *What Is to Be Done?* Lenin wrote of the need for the revolutionary party in Russia to become a disciplined cadre of insurrectionists who would carry the message to workers and peasants in Tsarist Russia and then make decisions for and act in the name of these workers and peasants. Lenin became convinced that workers, if left to their own devices, would rise only to a trade union level of consciousness and would rarely make the decisive step toward revolutionary activity unless given guidance from a dedicated elite who had developed the needed revolutionary perspective and discipline. One of Lenin's great critics in the debate over the capability of workers to make a revolution by themselves was Rosa Luxemburg. Although she addressed this issue in several of her writings, the most accessible of these can be found in *Rosa Luxemburg Speaks* edited by Mary-Alice Waters and published by Pathfinder Press in 1970. In general, Luxemburg felt that Lenin's position on what was called "the organizational problem" would result in the general suppression of democracy within Russian Social Democracy. Many, including Staughton Lynd, believe that she was correct and that this was a problem inherent in the nature of a vanguard party.

Waclaw Machajski

Another more sociological—and more cynical—critique of revolutionary Marxism-Leninism emerged. One of the earliest and one of the most obscure advocates of this view was the Russian revolutionary theorist Jan Waclaw Machajski (1866–1926).[1] Machajski was born in 1866 in the small town of Busk in that part of Poland controlled by the Russian Empire. According to Paul Avrich in his classic study, *The Russian Anarchists*, Machajski initially adopted, as a young student, a political philosophy blending socialism and Polish nationalism before abandoning this view for classical Marxism. In 1892, Machajski was arrested for trying to smuggle revolutionary literature from Switzerland into the Russian Empire. Sentenced to exile in Siberia, he remained there for twelve years, until his escape in 1903. During his exile, Machajski subjected Marxism to intensive scrutiny and came to the controversial conclusion that the socialist revolutionary movement was led by a "new class" of radical intellectuals who controlled the workers' movement by means of their superior education.[2]

In fragments of his book *The Intellectual Worker* that appeared in *The Making of Society*, edited by V. F. Calverton, Machajski asserted that just as the means of production was the capital of the capitalist class, so education was the invisible capital of the new emerging class of revolutionary intellectuals.[3] This capital called education would enable the intellectual to write and speak with persuasion and thus to dominate the unsophisticated manual workers who did not know how to express their grievances against the capitalist system.

While Machajski remained obscure, he did have one disciple, Max Nacht (1881–1973). Nacht, who wrote under the name Max Nomad, was born in the Austro-Hungarian Empire but emigrated to the United

States, where he wrote a series of cynical critiques of revolutionary figures, notably in *Rebels and Renegades* (New York, 1932) and *Aspects of Revolt* (New York, 1959). Several times in his works, Nacht wrote that the relationship between the radical intellectual and the worker parallels that "between the rider and his horse." However, others wrote about this relationship with less cynicism and more insight.

James Burnham

When former socialist James Burnham (1905–1987) wrote *The Managerial Revolution* (1940), he provoked a storm of criticism from the Left in the United States. While the Italian Marxist Bruno Rizzi (1901–1977) had anticipated many of Burnham's arguments in his book, *The Bureaucratisation of the World*, it is clear that Burnham did not know of Rizzi's writings when he wrote *The Managerial Revolution*.[4] A native of Chicago, Burnham attended Princeton and Oxford before helping to organize the American Workers Party in 1933. By the mid-1930s, Burnham was a comrade of Max Schachtman both in the Trotskyist Socialist Workers Party and later, after a split in the Workers Party. Burnham and Schachtman split with Leon Trotsky over the class nature of the Soviet Union (USSR) after the Russo-Finnish War in 1939. To orthodox Trotskyists, the USSR was a "deformed workers state" but still socialist in structure. Burnham and Schachtman disagreed, claiming that the USSR had ceased to have a socialist character and was simply a "bureaucratic collectivist" state.

Bureaucratic collectivism was the cornerstone of the analysis of the newly formed Workers Party founded by Schachtman and Burnham. Schachtman's essays on this subject appeared in book form in *The Bureaucratic Revolution* (1962). However, Burnham was already traveling a road that led him away from socialism altogether. In *The Managerial Revolution*, Burnham argued that certain bureaucratic tendencies existed in fascism, Stalinism, and New Deal collectivism. A new class of "managers," he asserted, had risen to guide these various forms of collectivism in the USSR, Italy, Germany, and the United States. Over his lifetime, Burnham's intellectual and political journey took him from the revolutionary socialism of Leon Trotsky to postwar conservatism. He became a regular contributor to the United States' leading conservative magazine, William F. Buckley's *National*

Review, in which Burnham wrote a regular column called "The Third World War." In 1964, he wrote a cold war book with the dramatic title *Suicide of the West.*

Robert Michels and E. P. Thompson

Another analyst of the bureaucratic tendencies of political organizations was German sociologist Robert Michels (1876–1936), who made his own political journey from the left wing of the SPD, from which he resigned in 1907, to the Italian Fascist Party of the 1920s. In 1911, Michels published *Political Parties* (1911), the classic study of the growth of bureaucracy in Germany's Social Democratic Party (SPD) and in its affiliated trade unions. Michels asserted that political parties and unions tend to grow by attracting to their respective banners supporters and followers who were not part of the original founding generation. Whereas members of the founding generation displayed idealism, selfless commitment, and revolutionary fervor, later recruits attracted by the growth of the SPD saw the party as much in terms of personal advancement as of ideological commitment. Michels also argued that party and union leaders tended to identify as much with the interests and needs of the ruling bureaucracy as with those of the rank-and-file membership. The leaders in many unions fear independent rank-and-file activism outside of the control of the ruling cadre.

In the writings of E. P. Thompson, especially the concept of warrens, Lynd found a possible strategic solution to Burnham's dilemma. In his essay, "Edward Thompson's Warrens," Lynd describes the problem that Burnham's analysis created for him at a very young age. "The problem of the transition from capitalism to socialism has nagged at and puzzled me all of my adult life," Lynd wrote. "Burnham argued that the bourgeois revolution occurred only after a long period during which bourgeois institutions had been built within feudal society. The position of the proletariat within capitalist society, he contended, was altogether different. The proletariat has no way to begin to create socialist economic institutions within capitalism. Hence, he concluded, there would be no socialist revolution."[5] Lynd wrestled with this dilemma—"Burnham's dilemma," he called it—for more than fifty years and found, we believe, two partial responses.

First, drawn to the writings of the British socialist E. P. Thompson, Lynd found in Thompson's book *Out of Apathy* three useful essays on the transition from capitalism to socialism. In one of them, Thompson provides the useful metaphor of the rabbit warren. He envisions a possible future in which the capitalist society is "warrened" by thousands of democratic counterinstitutions such as cooperatives, neighborhood committees, workplace councils, and local assemblies. These would gradually create (to quote a saying of Wobbly Ralph Chaplin's) the shape of a "new society within the shell of the old." From this growing popular infrastructure of democratic organizations would come the new socialist society.[6] According to Lynd's writings, the concept of warrening the old society in order to gradually give birth to a new one was a partial answer to Burnham's dilemma.

A second partial response to Burnham's dilemma may perhaps be drawn from another part of Burnham's thesis. Burnham felt that the collectivisms of the time—Stalinism, fascism, and the New Deal—signaled the rise of the bureaucratic state less by elected politicians or dictators than by managers and administrators. After the end of World War II and the defeat of fascism, the world seemed to embrace bureaucratic reform—social democracy in Western Europe and the New Frontier/Great Society in the United States. The new postwar world seemed to be dominated by large national corporations, large national labor organizations, an expanding public sector, and the growth of what conservative writer Russell Kirk called "behemoth state universities." Accompanying this was the growth of a military-industrial complex that brought business, labor, and government together to develop a system of weapons capable of destroying the world. The Soviet Union was embarking on its own military buildup, and most of the Left was involved in choosing up sides. The Communist movement held sway over much of the Western European Left as well as over several nationalist leaders in the developing world. This was opposed by a range of anti-Communist conservative and left-liberal intellectuals, such as Sidney Hook and Norman Thomas, who joined the anti-Communist advocacy group Congress for Cultural Freedom (CCF) in order to promote democratic ideals and to defend the United States.[7]

Dwight Macdonald and Ignazio Silone

However, another humanist-socialist Left began to coalesce in the late 1940s. It sought to steer a course separate from both superpowers and their supporters. This new political third camp influenced young Staughton

Lynd; later, in one of his books, he termed it "the first New Left."[8] Among the spokespersons for this new left were Dwight Macdonald and Ignazio Silone. However, it is important to note that, while both men contributed to a new socialist humanism after World War II, neither ever fully embraced the kind of third camp position that we often associate with the New Left of the early 1960s. The third camp position stated that a credible socialist left should oppose both capitalism and Communism.

Dwight Macdonald (1906–1982) was born and lived all of his life in New York City, although on many occasions he confessed that he never really liked living there. In his magazine, *Politics* (1942–1949), he invited the voices of many different men and women associated with the non-Stalinist left. His 1946 essay "The Root Is Man" is the best example of this new humanist internationalism. Macdonald was also associated with the CCF and later stated on several occasions that in the battle of the two superpowers, he "chose the West." Nevertheless, his independent radicalism of the 1940s expressed many of the themes and values that were later elements of the New Left.[9]

Ignazio Silone (1900–1978) was born and grew up in the desolate and mountainous Abruzzo region of Italy, which became the setting for his three famous novels. He joined the Italian Socialist Party and then, when the split occurred, became a member of the Italian Communist Party, rising to membership of its central committee before his break with the party and subsequent exile. While in exile in Switzerland, he began to work on *Fontamara* (1930), the first of the three novels forming the Abruzzo Trilogy along with *Bread and Wine* (1936) and *Seed Beneath the Snow* (1940). While *Fontamara,* which chronicles the exploitation and violent suppression of the inhabitants of a remote village in southern Italy, had an impact on the antifascist consciousness of many Western intellectuals, including Alfred Kazin, Malcolm Cowley, and Irving Howe, it was *Bread and Wine* that most influenced the postwar independent Left, including Lynd. [10]

Silone's intellectual and political journey continued, as he moved from Communism to democratic socialism and then embraced Christianity. At least one of his novels, *Bread and Wine,* was partially rewritten in the postwar years in order to address the author's new Christian worldview.

Pietro Spina

The central character of Silone's novel *Bread and Wine* is the antifascist revolutionary Pietro Spina, who is on the run from Mussolini's fascist police. Spina comes to the remote mountain region of Abruzzo and hides himself by assuming the identity of a Catholic priest, Don Paolo Spada. In the guise of the priest, Spina begins to relate to the *cafoni* (peasants and farmers) in a new way. Instead of exhorting them with Marxist abstractions, Spina finds himself relating to the *cafoni* by walking with them . . . by *accompanying* them. Their troubles become his as he counsels them and shares their burdens. However, although Silone had his character identify with the concerns and struggles of the peasantry, it is clear that he did not romanticize them. He found many of them to be harsh, cynical, and superstitious, and *Bread and Wine* is often seen through the lens of one man's disillusionment with Communism. Lynd saw something else. Pietro Spina (and Silone himself) embraced socialism while rejecting the party. In Lynd's interpretation of *Bread and Wine*, Silone was depicting a new way of seeking social change. Hence, for Lynd (and perhaps others), the notion of accompaniment offered politics in a new key.

There is another way to view the novel, however. Recently, some evidence has been uncovered suggesting that Ignazio Silone may have been a secret agent for Mussolini's fascist police. While this revelation (if true) should not detract from the power and moral clarity of Silone's novels, it might help explain the fact that Pietro Spina achieves much of his success with the *cafoni* through deception.[11] Spina sought to help the poor by pretending to be someone he was not—a priest.

Perhaps still another way to think about *Bread and Wine* is purely as a morality tale, since it is hardly credible that fascist police or paid informers would fail to notice the arrival in a poor, remote district of a stranger whose cover-up name of Paolo Spada is similar to that of the notorious revolutionary, Pietro Spina.

Accompaniment

Staughton Lynd's own journey to accompaniment came about through a lifelong effort to find a partial response to the dilemma posed by James Burnham in his book *The Managerial Revolution.* Through accompani-

Staughton Lynd's steady speaking style is evident in this photograph, taken on 20 March 2007. Kent State University Libraries. Special Collections and Archives.

ment, Lynd sought to carefully build horizontal relationships between the radical intellectual and the worker or between groups of workers or peasants or members of a community. However, both the Lynds would agree that their turn toward accompaniment was less a sharp break with their past commitments than simply a shift to a new way of honoring them. In the words of Staughton Lynd, "We embraced the idea of 'accompaniment' because it seemed to describe what we had already begun to experience in practice. In her work as a draft counselor (1965–1970), Alice had developed the concept of the 'two experts,' one the professional with expertise about law and regulation, and the other the counselee with a different kind of expertise gained through his or her life experience."[12]

Accompaniment, as practiced by the Lynds in their work, echoes the actions of Pietro Spina in Silone's novel, *Bread and Wine.* It can also be seen in the writings of advocates of liberation theology in Latin America in the 1980s, especially those of Salvadoran archbishop Oscar Romero. Staughton Lynd has written repeatedly about the contrast between accompaniment and the "organizing model," as expressed in union organizing or the civil rights movement. In the latter model, the organizer and his or her comrades hits town and organizes the common folk around a set of issues that are important to the locals. Then the organizer departs to pursue the next organizing project, leaving the locals on their own to try to figure out how to implement on a daily basis what they have been "taught" by the organizer, who is now long gone.

Accompaniment, in contrast, is a much more sober and perhaps mature form of activism. In this model, the radical must forego the excitement of dashing from one community to the next, living out of motel rooms, and trying to figure out how to relate to the locals so they can be "organized." Instead, he or she seeks to actually live in the community among the poor or among workers. The radical seeks to build a life among the poor or dispossessed and relates to them by providing them with a set of skills they do not have.

For example, Alice and Staughton Lynd have lived among workers in the area of Youngstown, Ohio, since 1976, offering to the workers and their families legal expertise to which most would not otherwise have ready access. Other radicals might become teachers, doctors, or social workers who identify with the struggles of working families. Rather than romanticizing working people (who are human with the same number of faults as the rest of us) the point is to simply say to workers: "Look, I come from the outside, so I will spare you the radical rhetoric about your nobility and historic mission. Instead, I will say that I have studied your struggle and I'd like to help. I've got some knowledge of the law and I can offer the following specific help to you if you would like it." In this way, the radical substitutes a specific set of skills in place of ideology and rhetoric in order to actually help workers solve their own problems. As radicals and locals work together on an issue that affects all workers, the locals gain self-confidence and self-awareness.

Macedonia

Both Alice and Staughton trace the root of their later belief in accompaniment to their relatively brief but meaningful experience living in the Macedonia Cooperative Community, located near Clarksville, Georgia, from 1953 to 1957. Educator Morris Mitchell founded Macedonia in 1938 on principles that included cooperative living, shared decision-making, and direct speaking with others. When the Lynds arrived in 1954, they embraced these values and were in turn influenced

Alice Lynd, like her husband
Staughton, has been a lifelong
advocate of working alongside
the rank and file as coexperts
in the spirit of accompaniment.
Kent State University Libraries.
Special Collections and Archives.

by them, practicing them for the rest of their lives. Alice and Staughton
have often spoken of their happiness at being part of the Macedonia
Cooperative Community, stating that they would have been willing
to commit the rest of their lives to living and working there had not
the community been split apart when a majority of the members embraced a form of fundamentalist Christianity. The Lynds could not
accept this new direction and refused to join those who became part
of the Society of Brothers (Bruderhof) in 1958. Macedonia's collapse
brought an end to Alice and Staughton's involvement in intentional
communities committed to values different from the world outside
and seeking to stand apart from mainstream society and become self-
supporting. As the 1950s drew to a close and as black Southerners began to strain against the bonds of Jim Crow, Alice and Staughton came
to see the growing civil rights movement in general and the SNCC in
particular as another way of achieving what they had lost through the
dissolution of Macedonia: a beloved community.

Staughton's effort to find a solution to Burnham's dilemma was
part of an intellectual journey that culminated in the decision by both

Lynds to move from Chicago to Youngstown in 1976 to begin an active phase of accompaniment in the service of workers, retirees, prisoners, and their families. The move toward accompaniment was, in part, an attempt to realize in a different form the rootedness, comradeship, and sense of place that they had found in the Macedonia Cooperative Community. An important accompaniment experience for Alice was the draft counseling work she did during the years of the Vietnam War. It is that experience to which we now turn.

Chapter Two ⌒◯

DRAFT COUNSELING AS ACCOMPANIMENT

"In draft counseling, there are two experts."

ALICE LYND

The Draft in American History

The issue of the conscription of American citizens to serve in the military has arisen several times in American history. The draft was first used during the Civil War, when the United States and later the Confederate States of America each passed conscription laws to guarantee the continued flow of men into the ranks of their armies as the war dragged on. The late James W. Geary, historian and librarian at Kent State University, detailed the implementation of the Union draft in his fine study, *We Need Men: The Union Draft in the Civil War* (1991). Both conscription efforts caused strenuous, and at sometimes violent, resistance.

When the United States entered World War I, President Woodrow Wilson elected to use the conscription of citizens as a way to bring young men into the army. In 1917, Congress passed the Selective Service Act, which updated the conscription system used during the Civil War. The enforcement and administration of the updated draft system created in 1917 was entrusted to the local draft boards found in county seats around the United States. John W. Chambers, in *To Raise an Army: The Draft Comes to Modern America* (1987), provides a useful overview of the draft in the twentieth century United States. Passage of the 1917 conscription law prompted legal challenges by activists on the left, such as anarchist Emma Goldman. The act also prompted violent protests such as the little-known Green Corn Rebellion (2–3 August 1917), which was centered in rural Pontotoc County in south-eastern Oklahoma. Participating in the armed uprising were poor tenant farmers, Seminoles, Creeks, African Americans, and activists from the Socialist Party of Oklahoma. The story of the rebellion is told in Garin Burbank's little book, *When the Farmers Voted Red: The Gospel of Socialism in the Oklahoma Countryside, 1910–1924* (1977). The suppression of the Green Corn Rebellion led to the decimation of the Socialist Party, which was strong in rural Oklahoma. This fact is often forgotten, since present-day Oklahoma is one of the most conservative and most reliably Republican states in the country.

In 1940, just before the United States entered World War II, a new draft law, the Selective Training and Service Act, was passed, based on the 1917 Selective Service Act and providing for the first peacetime draft in U.S. history. Once again, the draft prompted resistance by many groups and individuals opposed to the war. More than seventy thousand young men were granted status as conscientious objectors (COs) and the vast majority of these were assigned to work camps known as Civilian Public Service (CPS) camps. About six thousand young men refused to register for the draft and, as a result, faced trial and prison. A number of young pacifists who later became part of the movement against the Vietnam War in the 1960s began as draft resisters during World War II. These included Larry Gara, David Dellinger, and Bayard Rustin, as well as others associated with such organizations as the War Resisters League (WRL) and the Fellowship of Reconciliation (FOR). David Dellinger's book, *From Yale to Jail: The Life Story of a Moral Dissenter* (1993); and Larry Gara's compilation of oral histories of World War II draft resisters, *A Few Small Candles: War Resisters of World War II Tell Their Stories* (1999), tell the story of the lives of these resisters while in prison.

In the immediate postwar period, after terminating the wartime draft in 1947, Congress passed a new Selective Service Act in June 1948, which reestablished peacetime conscription. The WRL and other pacifist groups protested its passage, objecting not only to its peacetime nature but to the institution of a draft under any circumstances.

The 1948 act was amended after the outbreak of the Korean War, which began in 1950, so as to lower the draft age, raise the duration of active-duty service, and increase the statutory minimum of military service. When this conflict began, young Staughton Lynd was not yet twenty-one years of age. Staughton applied for a draft status as a conscientious objector and was granted draft classification of 1-A-O (CO status) in November 1953. Carl Mirra, in *The Admirable Radical: Staughton Lynd and Cold War Dissent, 1945–1970* (2010), details Staughton's assignment to a Medical Corps unit at a U.S. Army camp in Virginia. During Staughton's brief stay in the army, Alice lived in Chicago and worked at Roosevelt University. This was Alice's first experience with the military draft, and it would figure in her decision to become a draft counselor during the Vietnam War, when many young men faced the same agonizing choices that Staughton had faced in the early 1950s.

The Draft in the Vietnam War

Although only Alice worked as a trained draft counselor during the Vietnam War, both Alice and Staughton took part in the draft resistance movement during that era. In 1968, the two worked together to edit *We Won't Go: Personal Histories of War Objectors*. In addition, Staughton collaborated with antiwar activist Michael Ferber to write *The Resistance* (1971), a study of the resistance movement against the draft and the Vietnam War.

When the Johnson Administration began to escalate the United States' presence in Vietnam, a division developed within the peace community about just how to approach draft counseling. Old-line peace organizations, such as the American Friends Service Committee (AFSC) and the Committee for Nonviolent Action (CNVA), took a traditional approach, focused on helping potential draftees win classification as conscientious objectors. In a sense, this approach was much less political than the second approach in that it helped young men work within the existing draft system. More recent and radical groups, notably the SDS and such local draft resistance groups as the Wisconsin Draft Resistance Union (WDRU), took a different approach, however, focused on helping potential draftees avoid the draft by whatever means necessary, including outright deception. Since the catalyst for resistance was specifically the Vietnam War, many draft counselors concentrated their efforts on helping each young man obtain whatever deferment might be possible for him. It remains for Alice to describe her approach to draft counseling, allowing the reader to decide into which general category it might fall.

Alice as a Draft Counselor: The Two Experts

Alice Lynd became a draft counselor because of an incident occurring in 1965. "In the spring of 1965," she recalls, "a friend visited us who had met several Vietnamese women at a gathering in Asia sponsored by the Women's International League for Peace and Freedom. Our friend said that Vietnamese women would go out at night and talk with South Vietnamese soldiers, trying to persuade them to side with the villagers rather than fight."[1]

Alice related that she and Staughton attended the Assembly of Unrepresented People in Washington, D.C., in the summer of 1965. Various tents at the conference on the Washington Mall were manned by representatives of a variety of groups associated with the peace movement. At the booth for the Central Committee of Conscientious Objectors (CCCO), she spoke with a man about becoming a draft counselor. When she asked if she could become such a counselor, he responded: "Well I guess you could if you could get anyone to come to you. There is one woman who does it."[2] The Assembly of Unrepresented People, though often overlooked by those who write about the Vietnam period, actually represented a pivotal moment in the history of the antiwar movement. At the conclusion of the conference, a number of independent antiwar activists, including David Dellinger, civil rights activist Bob Moses, and Staughton Lynd, helped to set up the structure for the National Coordinating Committee to End the War in Vietnam (NCC). The NCC and successor organizations under different names coordinated the major demonstrations against the war.

Alice continued with the following observation: "We were living five blocks from Yale University at that time and students were frequently in and out of our apartment. I put up a little sign provided by the CCCO, with my name on it saying that draft counseling was available here."[3]

After Staughton Lynd lost his job as a history professor at Yale University, the Lynds moved from New Haven to Chicago's south side.[4] Alice recalled her draft counseling work in Chicago and her uneasy fit into some of the movement groups of the late 1960s.

> CADRE (Chicago Area Draft Resistance) . . . was up front. The resisters would say why they were resisting and would take the consequences.

We had in the late sixties when we moved to Chicago people who regarded themselves as part of the movement. [These people] assigned us to what they called a cell, where maybe eight or ten people would be expected to meet together on a regular basis. They thought what they were doing—or the important thing to do—was consciousness-raising. To my mind this was just winding the spring tighter without offering any solution. I did not like being a part of the cell [and] I did not like the cell to which we were assigned. It seemed to me quite irrelevant to what was needed.[5]

Alice felt that while she was working to help young men deal with the realistic options open to them in facing the draft, she was not necessarily part of what was often called "the movement," of which draft counseling was often seen to be a part.

Alice remembered the following experiences that affected her attitudes about the movement:

The women's movement was under way when we got to Chicago. I went to just a few meetings, and now and then a woman would come to see me, or I would have an invitation to go to some place. I remember one mother trying to convince me that I shouldn't go along with the subservience of women and the domination by men and so forth. But that wasn't my experience growing up. I had a very strong mother who insisted on being treated as an equal with my father. My father was a very gentle, gracious man. I mean it just didn't fit the stereotype. My mother, you know, had been a strong advocate of Women's Suffrage when she was a teenager. I remember being on the playground, with Heather Booth and her child and our child. I got the sense from her, the draft is a men's issue. Why are you working on a men's issue? Well, it's not a men's issue! It affects whole families. So I felt pretty disconnected from the movement as I saw it around me, and I decided not to be a part of it.[6]

For Alice, the draft counseling work that she did was more about helping young men in need and less about making a statement about the draft or other larger political questions related to the war in Vietnam. It was also about her search for community. Alice continued:

The dynamism of Alice Lynd is evident in her face in this image from the 1970s. Kent State University Libraries. Special Collections and Archives.

I was still trying to deal with our loss of the community in Macedonia. After Macedonia, I felt our task was to build community outside of that narrow context. I didn't think of myself so much as part of the movement as still trying to build community. As a draft counselor, in the late sixties, community was very important to me.

The concept that I developed of the two experts was like accompaniment. The counselor and counselee are two hands. The counselor brings expertise in the Selective Service procedures. The counselee is the expert in his own life and where he's been, what he's been dealing with, and where he wants to go. The two experts as equals.[7]

Alice Lynd's introduction to accompaniment came through her work as a draft counselor between 1965 and 1970. The experience of working with young men facing very difficult decisions about their futures and dealing with family pressures about service in Vietnam was very fulfilling to her. Looking back on this period, Alice remarked, "I loved draft counseling. I was meeting a person who was considering life-altering choices, bringing together what life meant to him, what his aspirations were for his future, what family pressures he was under, and what consequences he was willing to face. I felt awed and humbled by the depth of what these young men and their loved ones were willing to tell me. In later years, I wondered whether I could ever find such meaningful work again."[8]

Both Alice and her husband were strong and principled opponents of the Vietnam War, yet they expressed their opposition differently. For Alice, it was important to reach out to young draft-age men and their families and help them make significant decisions about the draft, military service, and the course of their lives. Alice regarded the process of working with each young man as a kind of accompaniment, in which she as the draft counselor and the potential draftee were both experts, working in partnership to find a solution that was morally acceptable to both. Over time, both Lynds discovered other tools that deepened their understanding of the principle of accompaniment.

Chapter Three ⌒◯

ORAL HISTORY FROM BELOW

"We must see history from the bottom up."

JESSE LEMISCH

Searching

By 1969, both Alice and Staughton were searching for ways to remain true to their values of nonviolence and participatory democracy at a time when what remained of the New Left had seemingly abandoned both. At issue for Staughton Lynd were the ever-louder calls by many in the Movement for violence against police and other representatives of the system and for a disciplined Marxist-Leninist vanguard party in the United States. It must have been a shock for the Lynds to witness the transformation of a movement characterized by the values expressed in the 1962 Port Huron Statement of the SDS and in early SNCC freedom songs about nonviolence into a current that glorified and romanticized top-down hierarchy and picking up the gun. In an interview with the Lynds, we asked Staughton, "In the 1960s you began to recognize features of what you would later call accompaniment. You related that there were several reasons why, after moving to Chicago in 1967, you began to feel at odds with antiwar and civil rights movements. How was your notion of accompaniment related to these feelings?"

Staughton outlined how the movement changed and how he and Alice found themselves estranged from some of its major organizations.

I would emphasize that it wasn't the civil rights and antiwar movements as such from which we came to feel increasingly separate. But rather it was the movement with a capital "M." SNCC was transformed into an affiliate of the Black Panthers. The Students for a Democratic Society fragmented into the Revolutionary Youth Movement, the Weathermen, and the Progressive Labor Party. I'd like to say what a good question this is because I think everything is contained in it. That is, if your project is to write about the Lynds in the Ohio years, it was because of the way we answered this question—that whole quarter-century or more of experience came about.[1]

It should be noted that while Alice and Staughton felt themselves to be outside the movement by 1970, they did not repudiate the values of the early movement—participatory democracy and nonviolence. By not repudiating the movement as a whole they avoided the long journey to the political right traveled by some one-time radicals, such as Ronald Radosh, Eugene Genovese, Peter Collier, and David Horowitz. In the 1990s, both Collier and Horowitz organized several "Second Thoughts" Conferences for former radicals who were in the process of making their peace with the status quo in American life and moving to the political right.[2]

All four of these former radicals pursued a journey similar to that begun by James Burnham in the 1940s. Burnham followed a path from Trotskyism through the Workers Party to *The Managerial Revolution* to the editorial pages of *National Review* by the time of that magazine's founding in 1955.

Moving from Yale University to the south side of Chicago did not make much difference in the academic career of Staughton Lynd. Denied tenure at Yale, Lynd found himself blacklisted from academic employment at several colleges and universities near Chicago. "My career as an academic historian was no longer open to me," Staughton recalled. "But the possible alternatives for full-time movement work available in the late 1960s and early 1970s seemed unacceptable. I found it embarrassing and shameful that the organizations created in the early hopeful years of the 1960s—first SNCC and then SDS—no longer existed ten years later."[3]

In two cases, university history departments in Illinois—those of the University of Illinois and Northern Illinois University—voted to offer Staughton teaching positions only to have those offers rescinded by the university administration. Then, when Staughton received what seemed a firm offer of an associate professorship from Chicago State University, the Lynds left New Haven and moved to Chicago only to find the offer rescinded; the state governing body of universities in Illinois had declared the offer to Staughton to be null and void.

History from Below

It was at this point that a decision to dramatically change the course of their lives led the Lynds to embrace a new framework for radical change as well as to move into new careers entirely. While their values remained the same, their approaches changed even before their move from Chicago to the Youngstown area of eastern Ohio. The methodology and human connectivity of oral history helped to set the stage for the next chapter in the lives of Alice and Staughton Lynd.

Throughout their long careers as activists and writers, Alice and Staughton have collaborated many times. However, the oral history

Staughton and Alice not only worked for and with everyday people, they became part of the fabric of their community. Staughton is pictured here laughing at a gathering of friends. Kent State University Libraries. Special Collections and Archives.

projects they undertook together are among the most important of their collaborative efforts. These projects, such as *Rank and File: Personal Histories by Working-Class Organizers* (1973) and *The New Rank and File* (2000), are among the best oral histories that have been compiled. In the late 1960s, Staughton Lynd and other New Left historians, including Jesse Lemisch and Howard Zinn, called for a new kind of social history . . . a "history from below."[4] This was history from the point of view of those men and women who played a role in great events that left few written records or papers, like the CIO organizing drives of the 1930s. Public history, the realm of museum and archives professionals, embraced the new social history and oral history as much-needed approaches to connecting people with their past.

Ed Wells

In April 2011, we interviewed Ed Wells in one of the reading rooms of the Youngstown-Mahoning County Public Library. Ed was a steward for Local 377, International Brotherhood of Teamsters, and participated in several struggles in the recent labor history of the Mahoning

Ed Wells was a young African American member of the Teamsters who needed help with workplace discrimination when he first met Staughton. Ed's father had been a worker at U.S. Steel, Ohio, and a loyal union man, and Ed grew up going to union meetings. Kent State University Libraries. Special Collections and Archives.

Valley. Ed has not written or preserved extensive papers, articles, or books on the events in which he took part. Yet he is not inarticulate—quite the opposite in fact. He is eloquent and perceptive in his observations of his community's labor struggles. Through his involvement in these struggles, he came to know the Lynds, both of whom he found willing to listen to and to value his experiences.[5] The primary method by which the insights and experiences of workers like Ed Wells are captured for students and researchers is oral history.

However, oral history as a methodology is not enough. In theory, one could compile an oral history composed of interviews solely with politicians, business people, and trade union leaders. These interviews may or may not be useful to those studying a particular period of history. However, such a limited range of oral history does not give voice to the rank-and-file worker, the waitress, the seamstress, or the secretary in a large office. Oral history must be combined with the ideological commitment to "history from below." One of the central goals of oral history is to record the experiences of those who are too often overlooked and later forgotten.

Staughton on Oral History

In 1992, Staughton Lynd spoke to the Oral History Association in Cleveland, Ohio. In his remarks, later published, he spoke of moving from recording the experiences of a worker to empowering that worker:

> There is a Spanish verb, *accompañar*, "to accompany." As used for example by Archbishop Oscar Romero in his last pastoral letter, accompaniment does *not* mean to disguise one's identity, nor to give up one's independent judgment and conscience. The priest or nun remains a priest or nun, not a *campesino* or a steelworker. The teacher still teaches, the lawyer is more needed than ever as an advocate. To accompany another person is to walk beside that person; to become a companion; to be present. In accompanying, the professionally-trained person chooses the world of poor and working people as a theater of action. By offering to tape-record the experience of poor and working people, we are implicitly saying: "Your life is important. It's worth my time to talk to you. It may be worth your time to talk to me. People like me need to know what people like you have learned."[6]

In his address before the Oral History Association, Lynd went on to identify five key aspects of the oral history partnership between the interviewer/recorder and the person or persons who are telling their story that allow oral history to become a tool in accompaniment.[7]

1. The interviewer and the person or persons with a story to tell meet as equals. This is what Alice Lynd means when she speaks of the "two experts" during a counseling session between a draft counselor and the young man facing the draft. Each has a level of expertise that the other does not possess. Thus, both are critical for the counseling session to work as it should. The same principle applies to the oral history encounter.

2. The primary purpose of an oral history encounter should not be to further the academic career or to enhance the publishing credentials of the interviewer. If either result takes place, that is fine. However, the primary purpose of the oral history encounter must be consistent with the ideology of "history from the bottom up." The main purpose is to give voice to those who have a story to tell but who have been overlooked or devalued by traditional research methods, which focus on leaders, public officials, and others with power and influence.

3. In the oral history encounter, the person or persons being interviewed often tell a story based solely on an individual or collective memory. These stories, no matter how faithfully told and no matter how well-organized, are bound to have errors and inaccuracies. Human memory—affected by age, illness, experience, print and broadcast media, repeated telling of the story, collective (group) memory, the transformative effect of time, and myriad other factors—is by its nature inaccurate. The interviewer can help make the oral history encounter more accurate by prompting the person or persons with a story to tell. Are the facts presented based on first-hand observation? Did the person telling his/her story get the information from another source the veracity of which cannot be verified?

4. While educated middle-class people may be individualistic, focusing on careers and small nuclear families, poor and working class people may identify much more closely with a group, whether it be an extended family, village, or fellow workers on the assembly line. As a result, the stories these people tell will often be less about

themselves and more about the group with which they identify (collective memory). It is the duty of the interviewer to respect the "ways of telling" of those being interviewed.

5. Oral history should be the story that the interviewee wishes to tell. This may be different than the way the interviewer wishes that it would be told. The person being interviewed is the one "doing oral history" not the person holding the recording device or posing the questions. In his 1992 address to the Oral History Association, Staughton saw oral history as a means of "giving voice" to the rank and file, to the poor, or to the powerless. It follows that oral history is or can be an element of accompaniment. Accompaniment is more than oral history done from the perspective of "history from the bottom up." It also involves a network of horizontal relationships among people in a neighborhood, town, village, or union local. It also means that the activist must commit to living in the community of the workers or peasants with whom she or he seeks to work. Finally, it means that the lives and troubles of the workers or peasants—not the implementation of a prepackaged political agenda or perspective direct from party headquarters or the college classroom—become the focus of the activist's work.

There are two lessons that we can learn from the work of Alice and Staughton in the area of oral history. First, oral history and history from below can be companions, but they are not the same thing. In the 1940s, some of the earliest efforts by historian Allan Nevins to interview participants in a historical event certainly qualified as "oral history." However, since most of the interviews were with members of the social, economic, and political elite, these interviews, however useful, do not qualify as history from below. Alice and Staughton, in their work with oral history, sought to allow marginalized people to tell about their experiences. Second, the Lynds sought to use oral history as a vehicle to reach those who were at the margins of society and thus unlikely to leave any other record than their memories of their experiences. However, they saw themselves as partners in the oral history process. Just as Alice saw herself as one of "two experts" in the draft counseling process, both Lynds tried to apply that same principle to the process of oral history. The interviewer is an expert in the methodology of oral history and perhaps, as a historian, an expert in some field of history. However, the interviewee is also an expert . . . in the experiences of his or her life that the interviewer wants to record and to use. Both the interviewer and interviewee learn from each other and are partners in a process. This is yet another form of accompaniment.

Chapter Four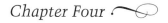

THE VIEW FROM THE SHOP FLOOR

"Your dog don't bark no more."

JESSIE REESE

Disillusionment

During the late 1960s, Alice and Staughton were increasingly disillusioned with the antiwar and civil rights movements. "I thought it was a very wrong direction," Staughton recalls, "to begin demonizing the foot soldiers of the other side by calling police officers and corrections officers 'pigs.' I did not think that 'pigs' was an improvement on 'niggers' or 'gooks' or all the other ways that human beings demonize those who disagree with them." The Lynds also disliked the undemocratic way decisions were made by groups like the SDS and others. As Staughton observed, "They caucused beforehand. The leaders decided what the correct line is, they proceeded mechanically without listening to anybody to push their resolutions, to meet their preconceived arguments. It is impossible in that kind of atmosphere to have the sharing of experimental practice that had up until then characterized the movement."[1]

Staughton's thoughts about the labor movement also changed in the late 1960s, influenced partly by his growing interest in accompaniment and by Alice's experience as a draft counselor. He explains that:

I began to form my own attitude toward the labor movement. I made up my mind that SDS and SNCC were being torn apart by a new wave of youthful revolutionaries: white, black, and Hispanic, in the name of the working class. I'm going to find out about this working class and I'm going to evaluate this hypothesis that the working class is the vanguard of the revolution. I want to make my own assessment as to whether in dealing with rank-and-file unionists you can use the language of the New Left about participatory democracy or whether you have to use some new Marxist, Leninist set of words in order to communicate.[2]

By 1970, Alice and Staughton Lynd found themselves at a cross-roads. The principal movement organizations, notably the SNCC and the SDS, had either transmogrified into something far removed from their founding principles or they had disintegrated altogether. The SNCC had abandoned its commitment to nonviolence and integration and embraced black nationalism, supporting the urban insurrections that swept many U.S. cities in the late 1960s. The values espoused by Stokely Carmichael and H. Rap Brown seemed to be leagues away from those advocated by an earlier SNCC leader, John Lewis, now a U.S. congressman for Georgia. In the end, the SNCC changed its name from Student Nonviolent Coordinating Committee to the Student National Coordinating Committee. However, its days were numbered; it had ceased to be the vital organization it was in the early 1960s.

The Students for a Democratic Society had changed as well. Moving away from the socialist-humanist values espoused in its founding document, the Port Huron Statement of 1962, the organization became a self-avowed revolutionary youth organization. At its 1969 convention, the SDS split into two factions. The larger, now named the Worker-Student Alliance (WSA), was led by Bob Avakian and was close to the Maoist Progressive Labor Party (PLP). The second faction, although somewhat smaller than the WSA, retained control of the SDS national office. It took the name the Revolutionary Youth Movement (RYM) and was led by Mark Rudd, Bernadette Dohrn, and John Jacobs. The core of this group would later become the Weathermen Underground. In a bit of political surrealism, the smaller RYM expelled the larger WSA, prompting the WSA-PLP supporters, led by Rudd and Dohrn, to reconvene at another location, claim their faction to be the genuine SDS, and plot a series of actions against "the ruling class" for the fall of 1969. Within ten years of its founding, the SDS was a shell, replacing the vibrancy of its early years with sectarianism and a caricature of revolutionary Marxism. The demise of both the SNCC and the SDS temporarily cut the Lynds adrift in the turbulent political waters of the late 1960s and early 1970s. They held fast to their values of participatory democracy, self-organization, and nonviolence. The problem was that they had no political home—and, as it would turn out, no job.

Blacklisted

With his appointment at Yale University's history department soon to expire with little or no chance of renewal, Staughton looked elsewhere for work. As noted earlier, he was recommended for employment by the departments of history at both the University of Illinois and Northern Illinois University, but in both cases, the recommendations were not approved by administrators farther up the chain of command. In a most amazing development, Chicago State University actually extended a written offer of employment. On this basis, Alice and Staughton moved from New Haven to Chicago's south side, where they rented a house. However, the Board of Governors, under right-wing pressure, voted to rescind the offer. As a result, the Lynds found themselves in Chicago while the reason they moved there had disappeared.

Luckily, Alice was able to find work. She secured a staff position in the office of the Chicago Regional Board of the Amalgamated Clothing Workers of America and then became a paralegal in a law office. Staughton considered working in a steel mill, and served as an organizer for the Industrial Areas Foundation, a community organizing network founded in 1940 by legendary organizer and writer Saul Alinsky (1909–1972). However, Staughton found that he disagreed with Alinsky's organizational premises. While Alinsky was an early biographer of the CIO and mineworker leader John L. Lewis, he is best known for his books on organizing, *Reveille for Radicals* (1946) and the much later work *Rules for Radicals* (1971), which was written in part to appeal to the sensibilities of the student left of the 1960s. Staughton found the Alinsky approach to organizing, which was staff-directed, to be quite different from his notion of accompaniment, which encouraged a long-term reciprocal relationship between the organizer and the community (whether of workers, peasants, or other dispossessed) that he or she sought to serve.

Seeking work in a steel mill or other type of factory was a popular tactic among many socialists at the time. Several Marxist-Leninist groups sent their college-educated members to get jobs in local factories or mills. How else were the proletariat to learn about surplus value?

This strategy was referred to as industrialization. Staughton considered working in a steel mill but rejected the idea because, as he said on many occasions, the workers in the mill would say to each other: "Let's go ask Staughton, the professor; he'll know the answer." In Staughton's mind, he would always be "the professor" until he had a set of skills that would allow him to relate to workers on an entirely different basis.

Perhaps Staughton could sign on for a job as a union staffer? What about working for the "progressive" opposition caucuses within some unions, such as the Steelworkers or Teachers? Leftists from many points along the socialist spectrum ended up working in these progressive opposition caucuses within unions. In some cases, these young leftists grew to enjoy the internal politics of the union more than the contact with ordinary workers, with whom they had difficulty relating because they had no shop floor experience. Staughton saw this lack of connection with the rank and file as tantamount to abandonment of the workers, and he grew suspicious of "insurgent" campaigns for union office. While in 1973 Staughton was involved to some degree in Ed Sadlowski's unsuccessful insurgent candidacy for president of the United Steel Workers, he generally felt that most insurgents, if successful, would simply control the bureaucratic machinery of the union administrative structure and use it for the same purpose as their predecessors: consolidation of power. Thus Staughton's values of participatory democracy, direct speaking, and commitment to horizontal working relationships, together with Alice's similar values and her experience of actually working on the staff of a local union in Chicago, prompted the Lynds to seek work together—work in which each of them would offer concrete skills to workers, rather than simply ideological passion and radical convictions.

"We won't go!"

As noted earlier, Alice found her work counseling potential draftees fulfilling in several ways. She was active in the Midwest Committee for Draft Counseling, an organization effectively advocating for young men facing the draft in Illinois and surrounding states. She also served as associate director of war-peace issues for the American Friends Service Committee. Her draft counseling experiences prompted Alice to collaborate with Staughton in editing a book on the experiences of Vietnam War draft resisters. The book, *We Won't Go: Personal Accounts of War Objectors,* was published by Beacon Press in 1968. Beacon Press is associated with the Unitarian-Universalist Association headquartered in Boston. The book was important to the Lynds for two reasons. First, it enabled them to make an important statement about the Vietnam War and the growing draft resistance movement in the United States. Second, it provided them with an opportunity to practice what they preached. Since both Staughton and Alice regarded oral history and "history from below" as useful tools in accompaniment, they saw great value in employing methods associated with both concepts to enable the draft resisters to speak for themselves and communicate what such resistance meant to them personally and to their families.

A Workshop for Writers

In 1969, Staughton met a young college teacher named Charles Mc-Collester. The first connection with McCollester may have been through Alice because Staughton remembered that she had worked with some of McCollester's students on draft counseling. Also, Mc-Collester remembers reading Staughton Lynd's article, "Guerilla History in Gary," and recalls that between 1969 and 1971, Staughton and Alice interviewed many rank-and-file workers in an informal group called the Writers' Workshop.

Before moving on to discuss the workshop itself, a word or two about Charles McCollester is in order. Since their meeting at the Writers' Workshop, Staughton, Alice, and Charlie McCollester have become friends, collaborators, and comrades. Like Marty Glaberman, another associate of the Lynds', McCollester seems to be a kind of worker-intellectual. He has a doctorate from the University of Louvain in Belgium, work experience as a machinist, and has served as chief steward with Local 610 of the United Electrical Workers Union (UE). He has been active in the field of labor education and directs the labor education program at Indiana University of Pennsylvania. McCollester also wrote a book, *The Point of Pittsburgh: Production and Struggle at the Forks of the Ohio* (2008), published by the Battle of Homestead Foundation. Together with singer and labor activist Mike Stout, McCollester collaborated with Alice and Staughton in several local struggles, including the Tri-State Conference on Steel, a coalition attempting to prevent the

Charlie McCollester has been a friend and coworker of the Lynds since the late 1960s, when he taught about labor and the rank and file at a community college. Kent State University Libraries. Special Collections and Archives.

closure of steel mills in the Pittsburgh area. Stout, himself a veteran of the Indochina Peace Campaign, a steelworker rank-and-file activist, and a folksinger, opened Steel Valley Printers in 1987. Both McCollester and Stout have described themselves more than once as "Staughton's disciples."

The Writers' Workshop, not affiliated with any college, offered workers a chance to describe their own experiences in the mill or factory.[3] Other workers shared their experiences and memories at a community forum held at St. Joseph's College. One of the results of these first oral history efforts by Alice and Staughton Lynd was the book *Rank and File: Personal Histories by Rank and File Organizers*. It is a collection of the experiences and recollections of rank-and-file activists such as Christine Ellis (Kate Hyndman), George Patterson, Stella Nowicki, Ed Mann, and John Barbero. Beacon Press, associated with the Unitarian Universalist Association headquartered in Boston, first published the book in 1973.

Another product of the Writers' Workshop was a twenty-page pamphlet entitled *Two Steel Contracts*, which was a critique of the Experimental Negotiating Agreement (ENA) negotiated between the Steelworkers Union and U.S. Steel. The pamphlet also included an imaginary contract based on the demands often voiced by rank-and-file caucuses. In the introduction, Staughton Lynd writes: "This is an imaginary contract, but it doesn't have to remain imaginary."[4] The pamphlet prompted a long distance call from Bill Litch in Youngstown, Ohio, in which Litch praised the pamphlet. In his 2012 book, *Accompanying: Pathways to Social Change*, Staughton remembers the following conversation with Bill Litch:

> With characteristic chutzpah, the Writers' Workshop decided to prepare an imaginary contract that contained only the more visionary demands. . . . I sent it to a group unknown to us, the Rank and File Team (RAFT) of Youngstown, Ohio.
>
> As the Lynds were sitting at supper a few nights later, the phone rang. A mighty voice bellowed into the receiver: "Hello. This is Bill Litch from Youngstown. What mill do you work in?" (Bill's voice, we

Vicki Starr (aka Stella Nowicki) is pictured here with her granddaughter. She was interviewed by Alice and Staughton for their landmark oral history of workers, *Rank and File*. Kent State University Libraries. Special Collections and Archives.

later learned, was unnaturally loud because he had been partially deaf-
ened in the mill.) I explained that I was a mere historian. "That's all
right," the big voice responded. "We liked your pamphlet."

Litch explained that a few days hence the Rank and File Team
would be picketing outside a fancy hotel in Washington, DC, where
company and national union negotiators would be holding their initial bargaining, or "sound off," session. I said that, by complete coin-
cidence, I would be in Washington that day. We agreed that I would
come to the hotel and join the picket line.[5]

One of the most important byproducts of the Writers' Workshop in
Gary was the beginning of a long friendship between the Lynds and two
rank-and-file steelworkers from the Youngstown area, Ed Mann and
John Barbero. Both men were socialists, antiwar activists, and commit-

Along with John Barbero, Ed Mann inspired Alice and Staughton to move
to Youngstown in the mid-1970s and become part of the community. Kent
State University Libraries. Special Collections and Archives.

ted to rank-and-file democracy. It was largely because of these two men that Alice and Staughton left Chicago to settle in the Youngstown area. Staughton offers the following recollection of meeting these two men after the picket line in Washington, D.C.:

> After a respectable period of picketing, we adjourned to a nearby coffee shop to get to know each other. Two of the small group identified themselves as Ed Mann and John Barbero. Both had been Marines in World War II. During the war, John had learned some Japanese as a guard at a prisoner of war camp, and after VJ Day married a young Japanese woman whom he brought back to Youngstown. Ed and John worked at the Brier Hill mill of Youngstown Sheet & Tube. They had both been active in the United Labor Party, a surprising fusion of Trotskyists and members of the IWW [Industrial Workers of the World] with a base in the Akron tire plants. It became clear that they believed in racial equality both in the mill and in the Youngstown community, where swimming pools were still segregated after World War II. They also were civil libertarians, socialists with a small "s," and opponents of both the Korean and Vietnam wars. As we talked, I had the feeling that I would probably never again meet two such workers. Over the next five years, we visited back and forth between Ohio and Illinois. In 1973, Ed Mann became president and John Barbero vice president of Local 1462, United Steelworkers of America, at Brier Hill. Thus they were strategically situated to respond to the closing of Youngstown's major steel mills and the resulting termination of ten thousand basic steel workers.[6]

Labor's Transformation

In the introduction to his book, *Labor's War at Home: The CIO in World War II* (2003), Nelson Lichtenstein describes an event occurring in August 1973, close to the time that Staughton, Charlie McCollester, Ed Mann, and John Barbero were working on labor issues. The event was a series of sit-down strikes that took place in the auto plants of the Chrysler Corporation in Detroit. These young strikers disrupted production at the auto plants, causing great consternation not only among the Chrysler executives but also among the leaders of the United Automobile Workers (UAW), even though many of them, ironically, had used the sit-down tactic in 1936 when the union won against General

Motors in Flint and other Michigan cities. On 16 August, more than one thousand union officials, staff representatives, and other supporters of the UAW leadership smashed the unauthorized strike and beat up some of the young strikers. This action by the UAW leadership, some of whom had socialist roots in the 1930s, seemed to demonstrate two things: First, it symbolized just how far the UAW had travelled from its "radical" roots in the 1930s. Second, it illustrated just how far many leftists had traveled since the 1930s in terms of how they viewed the labor movement.

Many UAW leaders of the 1970s began as socialist radicals in the 1930s. Over the decades since, these leaders made the transition from revolutionary socialism to social democracy (reformist socialism), with an emphasis on working within the Democratic Party. Many became supporters of Walter Reuther when he became president of the UAW in 1946. During the war years, much of the power once vested in the local rank and file had been transferred to the union bureaucracy, undermining or eliminating altogether the authority of shop stewards on the floor to settle grievances. Many social democratic activists said nothing when Reuther installed his own union machine, making the UAW a kind of "one-party state" for many years.

The social democrats also tended to cultivate trade union officials and to look askance at rank-and-file opposition caucuses within the union. Many took staff positions in unions like the UAW or the Steelworkers, aligning themselves with the ruling bureaucracy of the union. In his book, *1948: Harry Truman's Improbable Victory and the Year that Transformed America* (2011), David Pietrusza notes that Andrew Biemiller, former legislative director of the AFL-CIO, was once a member of the Socialist Party in Wisconsin before becoming a Democratic congressman for the state. Biemiller is but one example of the many one-time radicals who became part of the trade union bureaucracy.

Needless to say, the work of Staughton and his colleagues at the Writers' Workshop in Gary tended to offer another view. While the social democratic perspective emphasized labor's role in historic victories like the Voting Rights Act of 1965 or the 1963 March on Washington for Jobs and Freedom, Staughton's "history from the bottom up" view tended to see events through the eyes of the worker on the shop floor. What were the experiences of the older workers interviewed when the CIO began to organize their plants? How difficult is it to get a grievance processed?

Atlantic City Memories: 1964

Another critical issue changing the landscape for activists seeking to work with the rank-and-file worker was the shift in attitudes and affiliations between the older social democratic leadership and younger New Left radicals like Staughton Lynd and others. The social democrats were closely connected with the trade union leadership of the AFL-CIO and the UAW and with mainline civil rights organizations like the National Association for the Advancement of Colored People (NAACP). The young radicals tended to see the leadership of the AFL-CIO as part of the problem: it supported the war in Vietnam and helped promote U.S. foreign policy in some countries by lining up with local elites and opposing popular movements for radical change. Many young radicals who had been with SNCC in Mississippi (again including Staughton) also bitterly remembered what they considered the betrayal of the Mississippi Freedom Democratic Party (MFDP) at the 1964 Democratic Convention in Atlantic City. Here Walter Reuther of the UAW had demanded that the MFDP delegates give way to the lily-white delegates from the regular Democratic Party of Mississippi. The MFDP got only two "at-large" nonvoting delegates. In this way, Reuther and social democratic leaders like Bayard Rustin hoped to gain the support of segregationist Southern Democrats for the Lyndon Johnson-Hubert Humphrey ticket in the 1964 elections. SNCC activists such as Bob Moses and Staughton Lynd were angry and felt betrayed by what Moses called a "back of the bus" strategy.[7]

Vietnam: Social Democratic Dilemma

The war in Vietnam finally split the social democratic movement—to the extent that it was a movement rather than a grouping of letterhead organizations, such as the League for Industrial Democracy and the Youth Committee for Peace and Democracy in the Middle East. Social democrats like the UAW's international representative Carl Shier (1917–2007), writer Michael Harrington (1928–1989), and literary critic Irving Howe (1920–1993) were reaching out to some New Leftists as they struggled against the prowar faction within the Socialist Party that was associated with Max Schachtman (1904–1972), Bayard Rustin (1912–1987), Tom Kahn (1938–1992), Rochelle Horowitz, Penn Kemble (1941–2005), Joshua Muravchik, and Carl Gershman. Muravchik is now a neoconservative and fellow at the American Enterprise Institute, while Gershman, former assistant to UN Ambassador Jeanne Kirkpatrick in the Reagan administration, is now the director of the National Endowment for Democracy (NED).

It is ironic that Tom Kahn, Rochelle Horowitz, and Michael Harrington were members of Schachtman's Independent Socialist League. The ISL was the successor to the Workers Party, which had split from the Socialist Workers Party in 1940. The ISL merged with the Socialist Party USA (SPUSA) in 1958. Harrington, Kahn, and Horowitz all followed Schachtman in supporting a new strategy that they called "realignment." Schachtman, Harrington, and their comrades at the time (including all of those mentioned above, including Shier) theorized that social democrats should work inside the Democratic Party and drive out the conservative elements so that the Democrats would become a true party of the left and the GOP would become a true party of the right (which it seems to have accomplished). However, political differences emerged between Harrington and other former ISL comrades, centering largely on two issues: their stance on the Vietnam War and their determination of which forces within the Democratic Party deserved their support. Harrington and his allies (including Carl Shier) supported the liberal left of the Democratic Party and "progressive" unions like the UAW and the American Federation of State, County & Municipal Employees (AFSCME), while the other emerging faction (Schachtman and his allies) supported the war and allied themselves with the AFL-CIO leadership of George Meany and Lane Kirkland, as well as with such business unionists as I. W. Abel and, later, Lloyd McBride of the Steelworkers.

In 1972, these differences led the Socialist Party of the United States to split into three different organizations. The right wing (notably Bayard Rustin, Penn Kemble, and Carl Gershman) formed the Social Democrats USA (SDUSA). The center-left faction (notably Michael Harrington and Carl Shier) formed the Democratic Socialist Organizing Committee (DSOC) which would eventually become the Democratic Socialists of America (DSA). A third formation to come out of the old Socialist Party was the new Socialist Party, USA, led by the former socialist mayor of Milwaukee, Frank Zeidler (1912–2006), historian Virgil J. Vogel (1918–1994), and libertarian socialist and IWW activist Harry Siitonen. Unlike the first two groups, which supported different wings of the Democratic Party, the Zeidler-led formation en-

THE VIEW FROM THE SHOP FLOOR   39

gaged in independent political action and ran its own candidates for president, fielding Zeidler in 1976 and David McReynolds, a pacifist and WRL activist, in 2000. It should be noted that some members of the caucus that became Social Democrats USA supported Richard Nixon in 1972 and Ronald Reagan in 1980. Of the three offspring of the old Socialist Party, the right-wing Social Democrats USA is now defunct and was dropped by the Socialist International as a United States affiliate. The DSA remains the largest social democratic grouping today, with the "new" Socialist Party being much smaller.

There was no agreement between the followers of Harrington and Shier and New Leftists like Staughton except that they both supported the insurgent campaign of Ed Sadlowski for the presidency of the United Steelworkers of America. Social democratic leaders like Michael Harrington and Carl Shier accepted the existing trade union movement structure and philosophy as a given and simply worked to support the "reformers" against the more conservative leadership. As we will see, Staughton grew to question both the hierarchical nature of the union structure and the way in which power was continually centralized away from the shop floor and toward paid union staff.

One final word about American social democracy is in order. The social democratic right wing, led by the Social Democrats USA and union staffers such as Joel Freedman (Bricklayers) and Tom Kahn (special assistant to George Meany, AFL-CIO president) supported the more conservative campaign of Lloyd McBride (1916–1983) for president of the Steelworkers union over the insurgent Ed Sadlowski, who was supported by Shier and Harrington. McBride, the candidate of the AFL-CIO leadership, received substantial donations from paid union staffers who were dependent on him and the leadership for their jobs. This type of donation was later banned by the United Steelworkers of America (USWA). Over time, once the steel mills began to close, McBride's victory would prove to be a fateful one for rank-and-file steelworkers in Youngstown and the Mahoning Valley, and a long nightmare began.

Trade Unionism: An Alternate Vision

The May-June 2013 issue of *Against the Current*, the magazine of the socialist current Solidarity, carried an article paying tribute to UAW rank-and-file activist Jerry Tucker (1938–2012), who was one of the leaders of the UAW New Directions caucus. Although Staughton never

mentioned Jerry Tucker, he did on several occasions express his dis-
pleasure with "rank-and-file" caucuses like the New Directions Caucus within the USA because he felt that these caucuses, whatever their
initial intentions, simply ended up using the existing governing machinery of the union in making the radical changes.

A second critique offered by Staughton came as a direct result of his
work in Gary, Indiana, where he came into contact with rank-and-file
workers and with older workers who remembered a time when local
unions existed and were more effective and democratic than after the
later arrival of the bureaucracy of the CIO. One of those men was John
Sargent and another was Martin Glaberman:

> One of the people I discovered, I ran into in northern Indiana. He was
> the union representative who among the galaxy of people that I end-
> lessly admire, stands out above all the others. His name was John Sar-
> gent. He was the first president of the Steelworkers CIO local at Inland
> Steel in East Chicago, Indiana. Inland was an unusual steel company
> because it had only one mill. This mill employed eighteen thousand
> workers. John was its first president and I almost fell on the floor when
> this man told me, "Staughton, we had it better before we had a con-
> tract. Before the contract, if we had a problem in the mill somehow the
> open hearths would only produce half as much steel in the next shift."
> And he said, "we had more control over the situation."[8]

Worker-intellectual Martin Glaberman influenced Staughton with his
small pamphlet, *Punching Out.* In this pamphlet, Glaberman argues
that with grievance procedures and no-strike clauses and pages of "work
rules," the once-militant shop steward becomes "a cop for the boss."[9]

As a result of the lessons that Staughton learned from these rank-
and-file workers, he remained committed to the libertarian socialist
values held by the early New Left before the rise of Marxism-Leninism
within its ranks. Earlier in Staughton's life, he had been suspicious of
the leadership of the existing "international" unions because the leadership (characterized by George Meany) supported the Vietnam War and
U.S. involvement in the overthrow of left-leaning governments in Iran
(that of Mohammad Mossedegh in 1953), Guatemala (that of Jacobo Ár-
benz in 1954), Dominican Republic (that of Juan Bosch in 1965), and
Chile (that of Salvador Guillermo Allende in 1973). While he did not

drop this critique of the AFL-CIO leadership, Staughton moved, after the Gary, Indiana Writers' Workshop and after encounters with workers like Ed Mann, John Barbero, and John Sargent, to a critique of the entire trade union relationship with its rank-and-file membership.

Further Thoughts on Labor

Committed to workers' self-organization and rank-and-file democracy, Staughton saw the bureaucratization of the union as a process of separating the leadership from the rank and file, often causing the union leadership to see the rank-and-file membership as an inconvenience. Speaking to the centennial convention of the IWW in 2005, he had strong words for the existing labor leadership and the role of leftist intellectuals in supporting this leadership:

> As you know I am a historian. And what drives me almost to tears is the spectacle of generation after generation of radicals seeking to change the world by cozying up to popular union leaders. Communists did it in the 1930s, as Len DeCaux became the CIO's public relations man and Lee Pressman its general counsel. . . . Trotskyists and ex-Trotskyists in the second half of the twentieth century repeated this mistaken strategy with less excuse, providing intellectual services for the campaigns of Walter Reuther, Arnold Miller, Ed Sadlowski, and Ron Carey. Left intellectuals almost without exception hailed the elevation of John Sweeney to the presidency of the AFL-CIO in 1995. Professors formed an organization of sycophantic academics, and encouraged their students to become organizers under the direction of national union staffers. In a parody of Mississippi's "Freedom Summer," so-called "union summers" used the energy of young people but denied them any role in decisions.[10]

Alice Lynd likewise had experiences with unions that brought her to the view that, while unions were important to workers on the shop floor or at a worksite, the paid staff of the union often displayed values and actions that had nothing in common with workplace democracy. As she recalled in January 2011, "While living in Chicago and before moving to Youngstown, Ohio, I got a job working for the Chicago Regional Board of the Amalgamated Clothing Workers of America

(ACWA). I was told to write a history of the work that ACWA had done in setting up day-care centers for working families who were clothing workers. Although the work setting up day-care services for workers was quite impressive by the standards of the time, I was struck by the standard that nothing but victories and successes could be publicized in the union newsletter or in communications from the union."[11]

In the years since Alice had these experiences, matters have not changed much, according to Steve Early in his book, *The Civil Wars in U.S. Labor* (2011). Early analyses the Service Employees International Union (SEIU) under the presidency of Andrew Stern. According to Early, the SEIU put dissident locals in trusteeship, unilaterally "reorganized" local unions, raided other unions, and summoned the police to deal with dissident union members.[12] This highly critical study of SEIU stands in sharp contrast to other books, such as Don Stillman's largely uncritical look at the union, *Stronger Together* (2010).[13]

Over time, both Alice and Staughton became suspicious of trade union bureaucracies and the top-down method of governing international unions. It seems that many of today's "progressive" trade union leaders are simply glossy versions of the men described by C. Wright Mills in his 1948 book, *New Men of Power*.[14] The one difference is that now we have the new men and women of power, best exemplified by the leadership of the SEIU after 1996. When John Sweeney left the presidency of SEIU to assume the presidency of the AFL-CIO, Dick Cordtz, the SEIU's secretary-treasurer became interim president until the next SEIU convention in April 1996, when the delegates would select a new president. Rising to challenge Cordtz for the union presidency was Andrew Stern, who had come out of the Pennsylvania Social Services Union to become SEIU's director of organizing.

When Stern became a candidate, Cordtz fired him and locked him out of his office. Characterizing Cordtz as a "union politician of the old school," Stillman asserts that Andy Stern and those around him (Anna Burger, Mary Kay Henry, Tom Woodruff, and others) represented a "new breed" of trade union leader that would not employ the tactics of Cordtz and that would focus on the future with an emphasis on organizing. Shortly before the SEIU convention, Cordtz withdrew and Stern was elected to be the youngest president in SEIU history.[15]

Andrew Stern held the presidency for the next fourteen years. Stern, who graduated from the University of Pennsylvania in 1971, proceeded to institute a regime in the SEIU headquarters in Washington, D.C., that did indeed move away from the business unionism of the past. However, his regime moved toward a more all-encompassing corporate unionism, employing the vocabulary of the Wharton School, featuring terms like *density,* and *dues units,* and displaying a hostility to the old shop steward system. The Stern administration introduced "innovations" that distanced workers from the leadership. One of these was a call center where a worker, rather than talking to a steward who knew the contract, would instead telephone a distant call center where the call would be answered by a staffer who very likely knew almost nothing about the conditions at the worker's specific job site.

A final policy adopted by this new breed of labor leader was the decision to divide and reorganize strong independent locals so as to break up centers of resistance to the centralism coming out of SEIU headquarters in Washington, D.C. One of most egregious examples of this practice was the effort of SEIU leaders to place the California United Healthcare Workers West (UHW) under trusteeship—in other words, under the direct control of the SEIU national office. This misplaced effort by SEIU touched off a virtual civil war in the California health-care industry as dissident UHW workers met to create a new union to challenge the centralism of SEIU. The story of the creation of the National Union of Healthcare Workers (NUHW) is told in Cal Winslow's *Labor's Civil Wars in California* (2010).[16]

The shortcomings of the current leadership of SEIU (now headed by Mary Kay Henry after Stern's resignation) are not the central point here, but merely an example of the general shift in union management from local control to centralized bureaucracies neither inclined nor organized to encourage close communication with or direction from the rank and file. Such a shift is antithetical to the values of workers' self-organization and rank-and-file democracy held by the Lynds. In their eyes, the key to rebuilding the labor movement is movement from below, not "reforms" mandated from a union's central headquarters.

Labor Contractualism

Alice Lynd later witnessed the rebuilding of unions from below as a result of her work with the Visiting Nurses Association in Youngstown. She remembers:

Because we did not have a staff person from union headquarters, the women had to do all the work themselves. There were these little groups of two or three people who would meet and come back to the whole group and say what they had found out and what they recommended. So the bargaining demands emerged from the work of the women themselves. Once, management wanted to lay off two LPNs, but the women came up with a counter-proposal to have rotating layoffs so that no one permanently lost their job. Management accepted it. These women took on a lot of this kind of responsibility for their own lives. Management did not have to deal with people saying, "How come she got that time off" and so forth. That was the union's business and the women themselves worked these things out.[17]

While Alice and Staughton lived in Chicago, their attitudes toward unions and the labor movement were formed through several incidents and experiences. Initially, the Writers' Workshop in Gary helped Staughton to clarify his thinking on unions. Through it, for example, he met rank-and-file workers like steelworker John Sargent, who had been through the bitter organizing drives of the 1930s and remembered a time when workers controlled the shop floor, had the power to settle disputes on the spot, and were not hampered by the no-strike clause that became a standard feature of CIO labor agreements after the passage of the Wagner Act. As mentioned earlier, Sargent told Staughton that he felt workers had been better off before the rise of top-down CIO union bureaucracies.

A second experience influencing Staughton was meeting Marty Glaberman. While Staughton was still living in Chicago, before moving to the Youngstown area, friends gave him a copy of Glaberman's pamphlet *Punching Out*:

At the apartment of an interracial couple who lived in Hyde Park, Ken Lawrence and Pat Berg, I received a copy of a pamphlet by Marty Glaberman, *Punching Out*. If I have ever in my life had the experience of the scales falling from my eyes . . . I was blown away by that pamphlet, which was written in about 1950 by Marty and other members of Facing Reality, a small but potent group in the United States associated with C. L. R. James. It [the pamphlet] has a pretty powerful conclusion, but the essential analysis is that the understood objective of CIO unionism is a collective bargaining agreement negotiated on behalf of an appropriate bargaining unit. Marty asserts, and I have found it to be true—I have held the evidence in my hands—there almost does not exist a CIO contract without a no-strike clause.[18]

C. L. R. James (1901–1989) was a West Indian Marxist intellectual who came out of the Trotskyist Socialist Workers Party to start another organization, Facing Reality, which did not see itself as yet another vanguard party.

Through his interviews with labor activists like John Sargent and from his contact with the ideas of Marty Glaberman, C. L. R. James, and other thinkers, Staughton found his ideas on unions and workers taking shape even before the move to Youngstown, Ohio. Alice's contributions were drawn from her experiences working for unions like the Chicago Regional Board of the Amalgamated Clothing Workers of America. Together, the Lynds came to the following conclusions about unions and workers.

Unions were important for workers as long as they operated in the interests of those workers. In order to do this, a union should be accountable to and responsive to the concerns of workers at a given work site. Staughton today opposes labor contractualism in all its forms.[19]

Modern collective bargaining agreement was a mixed blessing. The union typically claimed to represent the worker, but with the automatic deduction of union dues from the worker's paycheck provided for in the contract, unions received funds from the worker on a regular basis without an obligation to have much contact with the worker. Staughton told Mark and Steve on many occasions that he favored the old system, under which a shop steward collected dues directly from the worker.

The inclusion of a no-strike clause in almost all collective bargaining agreements was a source of misgiving, since it removed an important tool from the hands of the worker. Staughton also contended that the removal of the right to strike during the life of a labor agreement was contrary to the intent of the authors of the Wagner Act in the years leading up to its passage in 1935. As he recalled,

It was in Chicago in the decade 1967–1976 that I read Marty Glaberman's pamphlet *Punching Out*, which included the dramatic analysis that the objective of trade union organizing in the thirties, namely union recognition and a written collective bargaining agreement, had in fact many ways tied the hands of the workers in solving their shop floor problems because those collective bargaining agreements invariably contained a no-strike clause. There almost does not exist a CIO contract without a no-strike clause. But [the] no-strike clause was an essential part of CIO contracts from the very first mimeograph contracts between [the] steelworkers organizing committee in steel, and the UAW in General Motors.[20]

The adoption of the union as the exclusive bargaining agent for the workers in a given shop, after the arrival of the CIO, altered the role of the shop steward. Before, the steward had operated as a militant advocate for rank-and-file workers; after the arrival of the CIO, the steward became an enforcer of the terms and conditions of the contract on the workers. For this reason, Staughton does not favor the "sole and exclusive" language in union recognition clauses in collective bargaining agreements. This "winner-take-all" tradition, which seems to be enshrined in the procedures of the National Labor Relations Board (NLRB), makes coalition bargaining rare if not impossible. It leaves unions that represent a minority (sometimes a large minority) of workers in a bargaining unit with little or no say and no role to play.

The "sole and exclusive" provision bestows on a union the right to claim to speak for *all* workers in bargaining the first contract. Since that union may have won a very narrow victory over another union in an NLRB election, the "sole and exclusive" language grants the winning union power that may not reflect political realities on the shop floor. On 22 March 2012, at a talk before labor educators in Pittsburgh, Staughton made the point several times that exclusive recognition does not always serve the interests of either the workers or workplace democracy.[21] Present to hear his remarks were both academic labor educators and union staff. Almost no one disagreed with his conclusion.

A final issue is the transmogrification of a movement of workers with potential into becoming a social movement beyond "narrow" shop floor issues. While Staughton and Alice were influenced by the memories and testimony of early CIO organizers and rank-and-file activists, this phenomenon continues. One of the most startling changes of this kind took place in the United Farmworkers of America (UFW) as it changed from a movement of poor field workers (the National

Farmworkers Association and later the United Farmworkers Organizing Committee) and organized into an affiliate of the AFL-CIO.

George Meany, when president of the AFL-CIO, wanted the UFW to become a business union more like its sometime competitor in the fields, the International Brotherhood of Teamsters (IBT). Eventually, despite protests to the contrary, this change did take place: the UFW became less a union of impoverished field workers and more a farmworker advocacy organization with its hands in a variety of commercial enterprises and, of course, in the California Democratic Party. The once-proud farmworker union became another business union, featuring purges of staff and a lack of internal democracy that belied the romantic image projected by the union and its charismatic leader, Cesar Chavez, to liberal groups, churches, and foundations. This sad evolution is documented in excruciating detail by Frank Bardacke in his book, *Trampling Out the Vintage* (2011).[22]

We have seen how Staughton and Alice formed their views on workers and the labor movement. Both Lynds continued to hold to the values and lessons learned at Macedonia and hoped to find new movements within which these communitarian values could be at least partially realized. While Alice found both meaning and a sense of accompaniment in her draft counseling work, the labor movement offered some hope to the Lynds after their experience of seeing both the SDS and the SNCC turn into their exact opposites in terms of both ideology and structure. With college teaching seemingly closed to him, Staughton entered law school in the fall of 1973.

Chapter Five ⌢⌢

TRANSITION — BECOMING LAWYERS

> "On this rock I will build my church."
>
> MATTHEW 16:18

Staughton Attends Law School

Staughton entered the University of Chicago Law School in 1973. Why law school? Alice and Staughton explain it this way:

> By 1973, Staughton had not been able to get a teaching job for six years. Alice had recently returned to work after two years of disability. She did not have the physical stamina to work with young children any more. Funding for her job and all similar jobs relating to child care had been cut by the Nixon administration. Alice had done well as a draft counselor, putting to use her ability to work with rules and regulations. Staughton could deal better with abstract ideas. We wanted to work together and we thought we had complementary abilities. We decided to go into law.[1]

Alice and Staughton decided that at this point in their lives, it would be best if Staughton entered law school first. These two people from middle-class backgrounds determined to "retool" themselves with a new set of skills that they could then offer to working people, who often could not afford such services or who were unable to navigate the myriad rules and regulations associated with most fields of the law. This approach stands in contrast to the policy of "industrialization" practiced by some socialist groups, in which college-educated radicals took jobs in factories, mills, or other shops in order to bring the message of revolution to the workers.

Staughton graduated from law school in 1976. During his years in law school, Alice worked as a paralegal. Her first job in the law was as a file clerk at the American Judicature Society. One of the law students working in the office suggested to Alice that she become a paralegal. During the summer of 1974, Alice enrolled in the paralegal program at Roosevelt University.[2]

When Alice finished the paralegal program, she got a job with a Chicago law firm. "Upon completion of the paralegal program," the Lynds recalled, "Alice applied for a job with lawyers who had defended draft refusers. Alice had a lovely little office where she was assigned to go through a hundred leases, all in tiny print, to find out what the deviations were from the standard lease agreement in connection with the sale of a shopping center. This was not what she had in mind doing! Her other work was keeping track of every date when any lawyer in the firm had to appear in court and every deadline for any document to be submitted."[3] Since this job was not what Alice had expected, she looked elsewhere, finally obtaining a paralegal position at a small law office specializing primarily in worker's compensation claims. Alice was quick to learn most of the details of setting up and running a small law office, in case that would be necessary in the near future.[4]

Once Staughton had qualified as a lawyer and Alice had become a trained paralegal assistant, the couple sought a work situation in which together they could offer their skills to working people.

Youngstown, Ohio

The proud industrial city of Youngstown lies about midway between Cleveland, Ohio, and Pittsburgh, Pennsylvania. At the time of the 1980 census, four years after the Lynds moved there, the city boasted a population of close to 115,500 people, of whom about 40 percent belonged to minority groups, primarily African Americans. An industrial and steel center, Youngstown has always been a strong union city. Just after World War I, part of the eastern portion of the city was burned down during a bitter strike, while in 1937, during the Little Steel Strike, some of the bitterest clashes between striking workers and police and company security officers occurred in Youngstown. Among its steel companies, the Campbell Works were owned by Youngstown Sheet and Tube until Campbell joined with the Jones and Laughlin Steel Company as a result of the merger of their parent companies. Jones and Laughlin also owned the Brier Hill Works. Finally, United States Steel owned two more mills: the Youngstown Works and the McDonald Works. The Mahoning River runs through Youngstown and provides water for the steel plants. In *The Fight Against Shutdowns* (1982), Staughton noted that Youngstown was for a time a place where the American dream seemed to have come true for working-class families.[5]

Both Staughton and Alice moved to Youngstown, where they obtained jobs as an attorney and paralegal respectively in the city's leading firm that handled labor law for area unions. Alice purchased a modest home for the family in the working-class suburb of Niles in May 1976, and the Lynds moved to the Youngstown area at the end of July. On more than one occasion, Staughton has remarked that this was the first home that he and Alice ever owned. Previously they had rented apartments (Cambridge; New Haven), had the use of an apartment in partial lieu of an academic salary (Atlanta), or rented a house (Chicago). Now, however, the Lynds were ready to settle in a community, buying property there and offering to it skills consistent with their values. Looking back on the move to Youngstown, Staughton recalled:

> There were two extraordinary guys, Ed Mann and John Barbero, and I just had the flash—I'm never going to meet people like this again. On this rock let me build my church. So it came about that Ed Mann's youngest son had gotten thrown out of high school for wearing long hair. He had gone to the local labor law firm, which took the case because they wanted to be on good terms with a prominent steelworker. Ed gave my resume to the head of the law firm, who had some Trotskyist inclinations somewhere in his distant past, as, indeed, did I. So I wound up being offered a job there as a lawyer, and Alice in the meantime had taken paralegal training in Chicago.[6]

It seemed a good fit: Staughton Lynd, newly minted attorney with a strong commitment to workers, and a law firm that had unions as its major clients. However, the fit was not perfect. In the first place, both Staughton and Alice identified with workers rather than with trade union leaders. Indeed, Staughton and Alice had already come to know Ed Mann, John Barbero, and Bill Litch of the Rank and File Team, a group opposed to the leadership of the United Steelworkers of America.

In the second place, Staughton was not about to take cases where he would be called upon to defend a union leadership against charges filed with the National Labor Relations Board by workers complaining that the union had failed to handle their grievances in a timely or appropriate manner. "One of the partners of the law firm looked at my resume," Staughton remembers, "and allowed that he had never seen a resume like this before. He hired me as an attorney and Alice as a paralegal . . . I have to say that from day one . . . I remember a luncheon, a rather elaborate luncheon in the manner of lawyers . . . I think the law partner and I both perceived that it might not work because the firm got its money from unions. I was into representing workers who were being inadequately represented by unions as well as mistreated by companies. I think we both saw how there could be problems."[7]

Despite such misgivings, Niles, Ohio, has remained the Lynds' home ever since. They still live in the house they bought in 1976. Alice remembers the search for the house:

> I was looking for a house. Because I couldn't drive, it had to be a house near a bus line. Our friend Ed Mann said, "Don't move to Hubbard because the schools are terrible." And our friend John Barbero said, "Well, move to Niles." So I was looking for something in Niles in order to be near the Barberos. I looked at all sorts of places. I kept having the feeling, why would anyone want to live in whatever house I was looking at? [laugh] I expected to get some old house, but the real estate agent said, "Let me show you a new house." She brought me here. The house had not been finished because the builder had gone bankrupt—they weren't going to finish it until there was a buyer. That meant it didn't have some other personality stamped on it.[8]

House on Timbers Court

Alice and Staughton have three children. The oldest, Barbara, is now a teacher who lives near her parents. Their son Lee, next in age, is now a scholar and academician, while their youngest is daughter Martha. Martha has worked with weaving cooperatives; she is married and has started a family in Guatemala. In 1976, Barbara was already out of the house and Lee, at age nineteen, was away at college for most of the year. That left Martha as the only child living at home.

Alice remembers visiting the house on Timbers Court in Niles that would become their home. It sits in a wooded setting and is located on a cul-de-sac with no through traffic.

> I looked out the windows. There were dogwoods blooming in the woods. There were children riding bikes around Timbers Court. I had the feeling when I saw the dogwood, wouldn't I like to see that when I get up in the morning? And there would be children for Martha to play with. I was down in the basement, it was late afternoon, and the sun was shining in the windows. It's a very large area; it's an undivided basement the size of the house and the ceiling was high enough. I thought, you could have a ping-pong table down here for the kids. It had these steel girders and wooden beams. It just looked like such an honest, simple construction. I thought, "I'm going to buy this house." The real estate agent was concerned about my buying the house without Staughton seeing it. I said, "Well, he'll like it."[9]

Staughton did like it, and so did their children. Since Lee Lynd was attending college elsewhere, he did not spend a great deal of time in the house, but he did make a very important contribution to it. "When we moved here, Lee looked around, then said: 'There's no fireplace.' In Chicago, we had a fireplace and on Sunday evenings we'd sit around the fireplace, maybe cook a steak over the fire, and have ice cream. This was the meal of the week. But there was no fireplace in the Niles house. So, at nineteen years old, Lee researched wood-burning stoves and how you install them and he found all the parts. He put a wood stove in the basement so we could sit down there on Sunday evenings and have our times together."[10]

Stan Weir

One of the dear departed comrades to whom the Lynds have dedicated this volume is Stan Weir (1921–2001). During the 1960s, many young radicals of many different political tendencies read and discussed his pamphlet, "A New Era of Labor Revolt" (1966).[11] Stan Weir was one of the founders of a small publishing enterprise called Singlejack Books, located in San Pedro, California. Singlejack published books by workers telling their experiences on the job. Staughton recalls Stan Weir and the birth of both Singlejack books and *Labor Law for the Rank and Filer.* "What he [Stan Weir] did in this period of his life was to create a little shoestring publishing company called Singlejack Books with another former longshoreman by the name of Robert Miles. . . . Stan wrote a very eloquent preface about how workers never describe their own life situations to each other and the commercial media couldn't be less interested."[12]

Staughton then went on to describe how *Labor Law for the Rank and Filer* came to be published:

> So Stan and Robert set about creating this series of publications. Stan said, "Well, Staughton, you've been to law school—you've been talking to me about rank-and-file workers. What I want you to do is to write a little handbook. It's going to be of a size that you can put it in your hip pocket or in your purse, and get it through the plant gate without anyone knowing you have it." It was to help workers understand modern labor law—not so much to use it as a weapon but rather to use it as a shield—so they'd hopefully keep their jobs while engaging in other kinds of self-activity—shop floor direct action. So I wrote *Labor Law for the Rank and Filer.*[13]

This pocket-sized volume was aimed at helping rank-and-file workers learn the basics of labor law and how to act as their own legal advocates.[14] In fact, the book offered the following advice to workers: "Our point of view is that whenever a problem can be solved without the help of a lawyer, do it. Besides being expensive the law takes a long time. It is written and administered by individuals who for the most part do not understand or sympathize with the experience of working people. Lawyers, like doctors, make their profession seem more mysterious than it really is. They use big words when short words would do just as well. They encourage workers to feel helpless unless a lawyer is representing them."[15] While this passage is taken from the second edition of *Labor Law for the Rank and Filer,* the first edition had language that, if not identical, conveyed the same spirit of workers thinking for themselves. Perhaps readers of the present book will not be surprised to learn that the law firm that employed Staughton and Alice was not happy with the sentiments expressed in this book. Indeed, the clients of this law firm—many of the union locals in the Youngstown area—did not share the avowed goal of teaching workers skills that would enable them to handle some of their issues directly on the shop floor, without calling in the grievance committee representative.

Most unions adhere to the "servicing model" of working with the rank and file. The tenets of this approach are described by Mike Parker and Martha Gruelle in their book *Democracy is Power* (1999): "In the servicing model, the member is not encouraged to get involved at all but to turn the grievance over to the 'expert.' Even in unions that seek membership mobilization, the servicing model of grievance handling prevails: members may be mobilized to act for certain grievance issues, but they take no leadership role—no responsibility or initiative."[16]

In his book *Restoring the Power of Unions* (2010), Julius Getman recalled his experience of teaching in a labor law/labor studies program to which workers could apply. Those who were accepted proved to be spirited and inquisitive, qualities that later made the leadership of their respective union locals uneasy. As a result, the union leadership insisted that in the future, *they* would choose which workers would qualify for the program.[17]

Staughton had a similar experience after moving to Chicago. In the summer of 1967, Roosevelt University offered him a job in its labor education program. Staughton read a book on the governance structure of the UAW that suggested to him a similarity with the government structure of the Soviet Union. Both the union and the country had one-party regimes. The program of the UAW administration was voted on, but only after it had been run past local leaderships so that a majority could be safely predicted. When Staughton suggested this parallel to his class, the man in charge of the labor education program said, "What a ridiculous idea!" A vote was taken and the students supported Staughton's idea 2 to 1. But Staughton was not invited to continue in the Roosevelt labor education program.

Getting Fired

What happened in the summer of 1978 was not inevitable, but it was likely to happen at some point. Staughton remembers the event as follows:

It was July 4, 1978, and Alice and I received from the publisher a box full of these little books [*Labor Law for the Rank and Filer*] that had just been published. Sooner or later it was going to come to the attention of the boss and so we had a choice. Should we wait until that happens or should we give it to the boss—take preemptive action as it were? Being Quakers, we decided, well, we'll give it to the boss. And so we invited the boss and his wife to dinner. After dinner we went into the living room and the boss sat on the couch and I presented him with the book. I was fired at ten o'clock the following morning.[18]

Was Staughton fired because of what he wrote in *Labor Law for the Rank and Filer*? Perhaps, but Staughton thinks it had more to do with union clients who were unhappy with his orientation to the rank and file. As he recalls, "This up and coming young law partner who is now head of the firm said that they had complaints from at least half a dozen unions about me. That's what was really going on."[19]

Alice continued to work for the law firm for another year, but she felt she was working for the clients, not for the law firm. It was about two years since the Lynds had left friends and commitments in Chicago to move to Youngstown and start a new chapter in their lives. Suddenly, Staughton had no job. There is an irony here, because Staughton had received job offers from at least three colleges in Illinois to teach history. The offers were extended by the various history departments of these institutions, but each offer was vetoed by the upper administrations of the respective schools. A major reason why Staughton had gone to law school in the first place was to help workers resolve problems themselves rather than hand over their power to leaders or administrators working from the top down. Yet such hierarchies had prevented him teaching in universities and now they had applied pressure that had cost him his first job as an attorney.

Before Staughton's dismissal from the Youngstown law firm, Bob Clyde, director of Northeast Ohio Legal Services (NOLS), had asked him to serve on that organization's board of directors. So now he called Clyde. According to Staughton, the conversation was brief:

I wasn't looking forward to the process of finding another job. But I called Bob Clyde, the director of [Northeast Ohio] Legal Services—and

I forget how I put it to him. I think I said something like could I have an appointment to see him. He said, "Staughton, are you looking for a job? You're hired!" I said, "Now, I do have one condition, Bob, which is I want to work only on employment law." He said, "That's fine." It was a pretty seamless transition. I worked at Northeast Ohio Legal Services from 1978 until Alice joined me there in 1985. We worked there until we both retired in 1996. . . . And basically we have worked as pro bono lawyers for the American Civil Liberties Union since.[20]

In the meantime, the law firm that had fired Staughton kept Alice on in her capacity as a paralegal. Alice had developed an expertise in Social Security disability, an area for which the firm had no one to replace her. One day, Martha was home from school sick and Alice obtained permission from the law firm to stay home and care for her. Staughton described his final encounter with his former employer:

Since the law firm and Legal Services were almost next door to each other in downtown Youngstown, Alice telephoned me and said, would I mind stopping by her office at the law firm and picking up such and such that she thought was on her desk, so she could work on it at home. So, I breezed into the law firm as if I owned the place–said good morning to the receptionist and went on back to Alice's office to get whatever it was she wanted me to pick up. There were a couple of Teamsters business agents sitting in the waiting area. One of them said, " . . . you can't keep this woman working here, because Staughton can just walk in and have access to anything he wants." So Alice was fired, forced out.[21]

After her dismissal by the same law firm that had earlier fired Staughton, Alice went to work for another private law firm that practiced in the area in which Alice was an expert: Social Security disability. One of the partners of the firm told Alice: "If you see that there isn't much money in a case, don't put much time into it." To this, Alice thought to herself: "If you ask me to take a case, I will do what the case requires."[22] Alice and Staughton always wished to work together, side by side in the practice of the law, to help working people. By 1982, six years after moving to Youngstown, they still had not accomplished this goal.

Alice Becomes a Lawyer

Several times, Staughton remarked on the fact that Alice prepared many briefs but only Staughton could sign them because Alice was not a lawyer. Staughton explored ways to have Alice become an attorney. It was not possible in Ohio or Pennsylvania for Alice to be admitted to practice law simply by taking the bar exam, so Alice applied for admission to the Law School of the University of Pittsburgh and was accepted into the class of students beginning in the fall of 1982. Alice and Staughton rented a one-room apartment near the law school where they slept during the week, and Alice came home to Ohio on weekends.

The following illustrates both the level of Alice's commitment to becoming an attorney and Staughton's commitment to helping Alice when he could:

> Preparing for exams at the end of her second year, Alice's hand became inflamed. The inflammation progressed to both hands over the summer. She could not write. She could not type. She could not slice bread or even a tomato. She returned for her third year at law school with a small tape recorder and a variety of small, colored, self-adhesive dots. Alice had an elaborate color code: as she read cases, she used one color for the facts, another color for the holdings, and so on. During class, if the professor made three points referring to a particular case, Alice would put three paper clips on the page in the textbook. After class, she would force herself to recall the three points and then speak into the tape recorder, summarizing what she needed to remember about that case. At exam time, she and Staughton were assigned a room where Alice dictated while Staughton typed her exams. Alice did better in her third year than ever before and graduated with honors.[23]

In January 1984, Alice walked into one of her law classes for that semester, Civil Rights Litigation. The course was taught by Professor Jules Lobel, who was also associated with the Center for Constitutional Rights (CCR), a legal advocacy organization that came out of the civil rights movement. At an interview on 11 September 2013, Jules Lobel fondly remembered his first meeting with Alice Lynd. He noted that it launched a thirty-year collaboration between himself and the Lynds.

The partnership was a natural because all three lawyers strongly believed in what Lobel called "prophetic litigation." This term means taking cases where the chances of winning may be slim but that involve an important issue of civil or human rights. Through his work with CCR, Lobel was used to taking movements or organizations as clients. This work differed from the civil liberties law practiced by the American Civil Liberties Union, which usually represented individuals or groups of individuals as clients.

In 1985, Alice joined Staughton as an attorney working for Northeast Ohio Legal Services. This meant that the Lynds were finally in a position to try to realize their accompaniment goal: for both of them to live in a community of working people while aiding them in their struggles by providing them with legal expertise that they otherwise might not easily obtain. As it happened, their achievement of this goal was very fortunate for the workers of Youngstown, since the city was facing the end of steel in the area.

In the nine years between moving to Youngstown in 1976 and Alice beginning work as a lawyer in 1985, life for the Lynds had changed in many ways. Both had become lawyers, Staughton first and Alice following nine years later. The couple had left Chicago and their many friends there to move to uncharted territory: the steel town of Youngstown, Ohio. In Youngstown, Staughton had become an attorney for a prominent local firm specializing in labor law and representing unions as clients. But Staughton's commitment to the values of participatory democracy and self organization, reinforced by many of the ideas of Stan Weir, ultimately led to his dismissal from the law firm. The firm's union clients didn't like Staughton's commitment to the rank-and-file worker, and the firm itself was unhappy about the advice Staughton gave workers in his first book, *Labor Law for the Rank And Filer* (commissioned by Weir's tiny publishing house, Singlejack Books), which encouraged workers to know the law for themselves and not simply to rely on the advice of attorneys. Staughton then joined Northeast Ohio Legal Services as an attorney, and Alice, newly qualified as an attorney herself, joined him there in 1985.

From this point until their retirement in 1996, the couple worked side by side at Northeast Ohio Legal Services. While friends and comrades in Youngstown, including Ed Mann and John Barbero, provided Staughton and Alice with a personal network of like-minded people, nothing could prepare them for the collapse of the steel economy of Youngstown, beginning in the late 1970s. This event would so fundamentally transform the working-class community that almost a half-century later, the community has still not recovered.

Chapter Six ⌒◯

THE FIGHT AGAINST THE SHUTDOWNS

"Why don't we just buy the damn place?"

GERALD DICKEY, STEELWORKER

Steel Town

Youngstown was a long-established industrial city when the Lynds moved there in 1976, with steel as its main industry and unions having a strong presence. However, the Lynds' arrival came just as the city's identity as a thriving steel town was coming under siege. Beginning in the late 1970s, global and national economic changes, including growing competition from foreign steel, a regional shift in manufacturing to the south, and growing automation, began to undermine the aging industries of the northeastern and central Atlantic states, rapidly transforming the region's "steel belt" into a "rust belt."

Youngstown, smack in the middle of this change, suffered a series of steel mill closures and a consequent rapid decline in population. Its 1980 population of just under 115,500 people (noted in chapter 4) already marked a decline from its 1930 peak, but beginning in 1977, the year after the Lynds arrived, both jobs and population declined sharply, so that today the population stands at about 66,000. In Staughton's words: "Youngstown had the unusual experience that the closing of a major mill was announced in each of three successive years, 1977, 1978, and 1979. By the summer of 1980, no steel was being made in the city."[1] This was a disaster. The steel mills directly provided about 15,000 jobs to Youngstown workers. They also indirectly underpinned a myriad related businesses employing yet more local workers, businesses that depended on functioning steel mills for their survival. In response, Staughton played a significant role in the efforts first of union workers and later of the Youngstown community as a whole to save at least a portion of Youngstown's steel production. While a comprehensive history of these struggles is out of place here,[2] we will examine Staughton's role in the efforts to save Youngstown's steel industry.

On 19 September 1977—a day that later became known as Black Monday—workers at those Youngstown area steel mills owned by the Lykes Corporation, a steamship company that had purchased Youngstown Sheet & Tube, learned in a company press release that the company's Campbell Works would be permanently closed and the company's steel production instead concentrated in the Indiana Harbor area near Chicago. The company's statement announced that five thousand workers in the local plants would lose their jobs. The union leaders present at this public announcement, including Ed Mann, were handed a written statement by company spokesperson Ronald Towns, who took no questions and then promptly left the room. The news came as a complete shock to the assembled union officials. Company officials had given no advance warning of the closures, let alone discussing their impact with workers or union representatives. In fact, the decision to close had been taken only the previous day, on 18 September, when executives of the Lykes Corporation had flown into Pittsburgh and held a meeting at the Pittsburgh airport, where they voted to close the Campbell Works plant. This was a unilateral decision by the Lykes Corporation,[3] one that would set off a chain of events over the next three years that would destroy much of the economy of Youngstown.

How important was steel production to the economy of Youngstown? Youngstown area steel mills dominated the land along the Mahoning River stretching from U.S. Steel's McDonald Works in the northwest to Sharon Steel's mills in Lowellville in the southeast, near the Pennsylvania border. Of these mills, the area's principal ones, with their parent companies, were:

Campbell Works—owned by Youngstown Sheet and Tube, a company then purchased by the Lykes Corporation
Brier Hill Works—owned by Jones and Laughlin Steel Company, which then merged with the Lykes Corporation
Lowellville, Ohio, works—owned by Sharon Steel
McDonald Works—owned by U.S. Steel

Ohio Works—owned by U.S. Steel
> Together the Ohio Works and the McDonald Works were known as the Youngstown Works

Struthers Works—owned by Youngstown Sheet and Tube, a company then purchased by the Lykes Corporation[4]

These steel mills were the area's dominant employers and consumers of materials and supplies. The concentration of steel production in the Youngstown area along the Mahoning River was considered to be "the greatest on earth."[5]

The Closings

The insatiable demand of steel mills for primary and secondary goods created many more related manufacturing industries in the area. Basic steel and related industries in the Youngstown area had grown to such an extent that on the eve of the first wave of shutdowns, about 80,000 men and women earned a paycheck from manufacturing. This meant a payroll of about $1.1 million.[6] Given this local dependence on the steels mills, the chain of closings that began on 19 September 1977, would be devastating over the next five or six years. Between 1977 and 1982, more than 50,000 jobs were lost in the Youngstown area. By the early 1980s, unemployment in Youngstown had risen above 20 percent, and by the end of the decade, as much as 40 percent of Youngstown's population was living below the poverty line.[7] Foreclosures and bankruptcies increased during the 1980s following the closure of the mills. As this book was being written in 2013, the percentage of persons whose income was below the so-called poverty level was 49.7 percent in Youngstown, the highest in any city in the United States.

Within a week after Lykes Corporation executives announced the closing of the Campbell Works, two clergy, Bishop James Burt of the Episcopal Diocese of Ohio and Bishop James Malone of the Catholic Diocese of Youngstown, with the able assistance of the Reverend Chuck Rawlings of Cleveland, initiated a series of meetings with fellow clergy and with community and labor activists about the plant shutdowns.[8] These meetings would lead to the formation of the Ecumenical Coalition of the Mahoning Valley.

However, an even more immediate response was the petition drive initiated by a group of steelworkers, including the union's district director, Frank Leseganich, and Gerald Dickey, recording secretary of Steelworkers Local 1462. In just a few days, volunteers gathered 110,000 signatures on the petitions. The petitions, addressed to President Jimmy Carter and members of Congress, called upon the government to take the following actions to save the jobs of Mahoning Valley steel workers:

1. Impose national quotas on imported steel.
2. Relax Environmental Protection Agency (EPA) standards on the steel industry.
3. Allow the American steel industry to realize a fair profit.

It is surprising, perhaps, to realize that this petition was actually written by union officials; steelworker activist Gerald Dickey noted that it could have been written by the top management of the steel industry. More than two hundred steelworkers took the petitions to Washington, only to be turned away at the gates of the White House. The result of this—the first of many futile efforts to appeal to government officials in Washington, D.C.—was that some workers, at least, began to reassess what the most effective course of action might be. Rank-and-file activists like Ed Mann and John Barbero noted that it was officials of the steel companies, not the U.S. government, that had ordered the closure of the mills. The decision to close the Campbell Works had been made by officials of the Lykes Corporation: they controlled this steel company and had decided its future. The rank-and-file activists and their community supporters realized that a more effective response to the shutdowns might proceed along the following two lines:

1. to mobilize the union rank and file *and* the communities of Youngstown and the smaller towns and cities along the Mahoning River valley;
2. to propose a concrete alternative to the existing model of the steel mill—that is, the steel mill as the property of a single company with the power to threaten, unilaterally and on short notice, the jobs of thousands of steelworkers and workers in related businesses and industries.

Behind these two plans was a more fundamental idea, articulated often by rank-and-file activists such as Mann, Barbero, and Staughton Lynd. This idea was that the steel industry was vital to the economic well-being of the Mahoning Valley and could not simply be allowed to withdraw without any concern for the impact that such a decision would have on the workers and families of the valley. Further, the activists concluded that since steelmaking as a private capitalist enterprise was gradually being abandoned in the Mahoning Valley, workers and their supporters should consider alternative forms of ownership to preserve at least some of area's the steel-making jobs. At a meeting on 25 September 1977, and at several ensuing meetings, residents and workers, among them Gerald Dickey, advocated the opening of a steel mill owned by the workers and the community. The concept was vague at first but gradually, as the idea gained momentum, it began to take practical shape.[9]

Criticism came from two sources. First, many on the left denounced the idea of a worker- or community-owned steel mill in Youngstown because they viewed it as a dead end and because they felt it did not contribute to the building of a revolutionary consciousness among Youngstown's workers. Of course, it was relatively easy for these ideologues to attack the struggles of workers in a struggling city who were trying to find some way to save their jobs; such critics could simply have their say and then go home at the end of the day to their own homes and jobs. Such a stance, when the leftist looks at such an effort as the Youngstown campaign and then attacks it on some theoretical basis, could be said to epitomize sectarianism.

The second source of criticism came from business union leaders such as Lloyd McBride, president of the United Steelworkers of America. Schooled in the approach to trade unionism that followed the 1947 passage of the Taft-Hartley Act, which conceded to the company the right to make all decisions about conducting its business, these business unionists often identified more with their corporate counterparts than with the workers they supposedly represented. In line with this position, they exhibited several characteristics. First, they opposed any initiative that they did not control. When McBride finally visited Youngstown, for example, he led his entourage in a walkout from a meeting during which the Ecumenical Coalition and consultant Gar Alperovitz presented the idea of a community-owned steel mill. Since the idea wasn't his, why should he stay around and listen to it? Second, they often accepted the company view that the government, not management, was the real culprit. They would roundly denounce imported steel, onerous environmental regulations, or some other factor that would gently lift the mantle of responsibility from the shoulders of management, where it belonged, and place it about the neck of federal officials in Washington, D.C. Government often does pursue policies that undermine jobs, but the point that these business union leaders refused to acknowledge is that the decision to close a steel plant is taken not on Capitol Hill but in the boardroom of its parent company. Finally, many of these leaders surrounded themselves with staff who simply agreed with them and offered no constructive alternative. Such leaders, insensitive to the impact of job loss among the rank and file, often seemed primarily concerned with retaining their own union positions and with identifying potential rivals within the union.

The Lynds' response to the crisis facing Youngstown was very different from both of these viewpoints. As their ideas on accompaniment began to evolve, the Lynds felt that what was needed was to walk alongside the workers and families of Youngstown as they struggled to find ways to respond to the shutdowns that threatened their way of life and their future. Staughton, in particular, drew on his training as a historian and an attorney to provide advice and useful contacts with other groups and individuals, especially after the Ecumenical Coalition was founded and began to function. Alice has sometimes denied contributing to the struggle to save the mills, saying she was busy raising her youngest child, Martha. But by tending to Martha's needs and providing loving support for her husband's work—work that was not, after all, warmly supported in all quarters—Alice made Staughton's involvement possible.

The Ecumenical Coalition

The Ecumenical Coalition was founded on 28 and 29 October 1977, at a meeting in one of Youngstown's churches, and its primary goal soon came to be community-employee ownership of a steel mill. Staughton served as a lead counsel to the Ecumenical Coalition. He recalls that initially it was not a matter of a huge groundswell of popular support for the idea of such community-employee ownership, but rather that no one presented any other ideas. "The idea of employee ownership made headway," he wrote, " . . . because no one had an alternative. I remember a meeting of steelworkers in my basement [at] about that time. Those present included Marvin Weinstock, who ran for national office in the Steelworkers Union; Joe Sims, an experienced committeeman from the Campbell Works; Ed Mann; John Barbero; and Gerald Dickey. Nobody had anything to suggest except Dickey. Dickey was the only person who had any notion about something to do."[10] Dickey became a tireless advocate for community-employee ownership of the steel mill, talking about the issue with friends and fellow workers and writing about it in the *Brier Hill Unionist*, the newsletter of Steelworkers Local 1462.[11]

One of the most visionary speeches made to the Ecumenical Coalition was given by historian and economist Gar Alperovitz of the National Center for Economic Alternatives.[12] Alperovitz advocated a worker-community ownership model for one or more of Youngstown's steel mills. His proposal called for two principal strategies: The first was a campaign to save the Mahoning Valley by mobilizing Youngstown's citizens to create "Save Our Valley" accounts at local banks. This money was to be invested in stock of the new employee- and community-owned steel company, if and when a new company emerged. The second strategy was an effort to obtain financial support from the federal government for a well-defined project to save jobs in the Mahoning Valley.

The founding conference of what became known as the Ecumenical Coalition took several important steps. Initially, the conference formally but reluctantly endorsed Gerald Dickey's idea of worker-community ownership of the doomed Campbell Works owned by Youngstown Sheet & Tube. The coalition decided to sponsor a feasibility study on the acquisition and operation of the Campbell facility by a community and worker group or the conversion of the property to some other use.[13] Reverend John Sharick of the Eastminister Presbytery, who served on the executive committee of the coalition, remembers that many in the coalition felt that a worker- and community-owned steel mill was "impractical" but saw the plan as the only alternative to simply accepting the closing of the mills.[14] While only three or four leading clergy formed the original executive committee, its membership was expanded by early 1978 to include many more religious leaders as well as community activists. Staughton Lynd joined the board as the general counsel to the coalition.

The Save Our Valley Campaign was formally inaugurated in February 1978, even though it had been active for several months. The key issue was the feasibility and viability of the community-worker-owned model for steel production in a capitalist economy. However, the key element of the coalition's program was the proposal for "community steel." While this model may have seemed impractical to some and too radical to others, important elements of the community did mobilize behind the idea.

Why? Staughton cited the reasons. First, there was the small issue of economic hardship, which often opens people's minds to new ideas. As he put it, "I do not deny that the presence of John Barbero, Ed Mann, Charlie McCollester, Mike Stout, and for that matter Staughton Lynd, helped shape the ideas that were brought forward. But we would not have gotten anywhere had the mills not first been shut down."[15] Second, the actions of company officials in announcing the steel mill closures with no warning and no discussion had discredited the model of corporate ownership of industry. Workers and their families felt compelled to explore more radical alternatives.

Union Leaders Respond

The pragmatism of the workers of Youngstown and their families did not extend to the local or national leadership of the United Steelworkers of America, however. The local district director of the United Steelworkers of America (USWA), Frank Leseganich, did not respond favorably when Gerald Dickey asked, "Why don't we buy the damn place?" And at the national level, Lloyd McBride, president of the Steelworkers, rebuked local steelworkers for their attitude, saying, "We can't tell a company how to run its business." On 20 September 1977, the day after the Lykes Corporation announced the shutdown of the Campbell Works mill, McBride testified before Congress with a perspective almost identical to that of industry officials, asserting that imported steel was to blame for the shutdown of steel mills and demanding import quotas on steel from nations like Japan. Staughton

Lynd further recalls that "when the busloads [of steelworkers] from Youngstown arrived in Washington on September 23, several rank and filers succeeded in seeing McBride, who had remained in the city for a legislative conference. He told them, as they reported his remarks, that the closing of a steel mill was like the closing of a corner grocery and that there was nothing to be done about it. McBride did not even visit Youngstown, about 75 miles from the international union head-quarters in downtown Pittsburgh, for more than six months."[16]

In *Steeples and Stacks,* Fuechtmann offers the following analysis of why the international union adopted what he calls a "low profile" during the Youngstown steel crisis:

> Recent politics within the USWA was also part of the background of the low profile adopted by the union hierarchy toward the situation in Youngstown. The international steelworkers union had held its presidential election just five months before the Sheet & Tube shut-down. Although District Director Leseganich had backed McBride, other Youngstown union officials had supported the campaign of Ed Sadlowski, leader of an insurgent faction based in South Chicago. In the union election of April 29, 1977, the Youngstown district gave Sadlowski 58.6% of its vote. Only Sadlowski's home district, South Chicago, gave him a higher margin. Opposition to McBride was es-pecially strong in the Brier Hill local, where Ed Mann was president. Attorney for the Brier Hill union was Staughton Lynd—socialist, an-tiwar activist, and now labor lawyer. Lynd was known, and strongly disliked, in the Pittsburgh headquarters for previous efforts on behalf of Sadlowski and steelworkers in South Chicago.
>
> A consistent position of the Youngstown rank and file was that they wanted jobs not benefits. When it appeared that union officials would represent their interests in receiving what they considered akin to 'welfare,' but not recovering their jobs, steelworkers began to look elsewhere. Lower-level union officials (the vice presidents, secretar-ies, treasurers, and grievance committeemen) from the local unions began getting together to discuss the situation. Staughton Lynd be-came a part of these often informal meetings, as did a number of Youngstown clergy. In these discussions in particular, it became clear that the workers' initial reaction to the shutdown—blaming Wash-ington—was only partly justified. And it was at one of the meetings,

that Gerald Dickey, editor of the *Brier Hill Unionist* and Recording Secretary of USWA Local 1462, first voiced the suggestion "Let's buy the damn mill and run it ourselves."[17]

As Fuechtmann notes, the internal politics of the USWA definitely played a role in the attitude of the union leadership. McBride had succeeded I. W. Abel as president of the Steelworkers, beating back a challenge from a reform slate headed by Ed Sadlowski. McBride had prevailed in a hard-fought election in which his opponent actually carried a majority of votes from working steelworkers. Once in office, McBride demonstrated his commitment to the business union perspective of his predecessor, who had negotiated the Experimental Negotiating Agreement (ENA), in which the union gave up the right to strike at the end of the contract.

In April 1978, McBride finally visited Youngstown to attend a meeting in which the findings of the feasibility study were to be discussed. After speaking for a few minutes to the assemblage of workers and community members, McBride became angry at a question from the audience and led a walkout of the USWA leaders from the meeting. Gar Alperovitz was then left to present the plan to the remaining attendees. The USWA even refused Staughton's request to file a friend of the court (amicus) brief, supporting the coalition's appeal from Judge Lambros's decision, in the Sixth Circuit Court of Appeals. Later, after first trying to ignore the proposal for a community-owned mill and after Red-baiting Staughton Lynd and Gar Alperovitz, the USWA leadership finally did endorse the community steel proposal. By that time, however, it was too late for the USWA's political support (such as it was) to do any good. Some observers expected that the USWA would offer its own plan to save the steel mills from closing. On more than one occasion, McBride actually hinted that such a plan was in the works. However, no plan was ever presented by the international union.

In the early 1980s, considerable discussion occurred among supporters of the labor movement on the wisdom of a worker- and community-owned mill in Youngstown. In November 1982, for example, such discussion took place at the first labor history conference sponsored by the Greater Cleveland Labor History Society, held on the Metropolitan Campus of Cuyahoga Community College, near downtown Cleveland. A local labor historian supported the criticisms of both the orthodox left and the business union leadership, citing the many unhappy experiences with "producers cooperatives" advocated by, among other organizations, the Knights of Labor under Terrence V. Powderly. An elderly veteran of the IWW responded that community steel in Youngstown was not a nineteenth-century cooperative and that, as usual, workers look (mistakenly in his view) to the international union for leadership and get nothing for their trouble.[18]

As noted earlier, the decision by the Lykes Corporation to close the Campbell Works mill was followed the next day, 19 September 1977, by its announcement to the workers. It was only later in the fall of that year that members of the Ecumenical Coalition and the Youngstown community became aware of merger talks between the Lykes Corporation and LTV Steel, owned by the Ling-Temco-Vought conglomerate (LTV). In the interim, coalition negotiators had tried to get from Lykes a firm price for the closed Campbell Works plant. In Congress, two Democratic senators, Edward Kennedy of Massachusetts and Howard Metzenbaum of Ohio, tried to pressure Lykes to name a price for the Campbell Works under threat that the senators would work to hold up the proposed Lykes-LTV merger by contacting the Federal Trade Commission. For his efforts, Senator Kennedy received an angry letter from Attorney General Griffin Bell dated 13 November 1978. In part, it read, "What you are advocating is that an administrative agency review a decision made by the Attorney General during the course of discharging his responsibilities as the nation's chief law enforcement official. If this evidences your concern over my ability to discharge my responsibilities, such an attitude will have unfortunate implications for effective future cooperation between us."[19]

The Kennedy tactic seemed to work: LTV named a price of $16 million for the closed Campbell Works.[20] This seemed to be a hopeful sign. In November 1978, the feasibility study completed by Gar Alperovitz's National Center for Economic Alternatives (NCEA) estimated that $245 million would be needed to update and reopen the Campbell Works mill.[21] To do so under worker and community ownership, federal loan guarantees for $100 million would be critical. Then in March 1979, the Department of Commerce turned down the request for $100 million in loan guarantees. With the closing of the Campbell Works, the EC became inactive after the clergy leadership resigned. The coalition had failed to save the mills in the Mahoning Valley.

However, it had succeeded, against considerable odds, in bringing some measure of hope and unity to a community that was both demoralized and badly divided. In their book, *SteelTown U.S.A.*, Sherry Lee Linkon and John Russo, codirectors of the Center for Working-Class Studies at Youngstown State University, write the following about the coalition:

> Community response to the mill closings reflects important aspects of Youngstown's history. The city's churches, many of which were the focal points for the area's ethnic communities, and the most militant members of the local labor community almost immediately began to organize. Church and labor leaders organized the Ecumenical Coalition of the Mahoning Valley. With assistance from Attorney Staughton Lynd and Gar Alperovitz, director of the National Center for Economic Alternatives, the coalition established local and national research networks, organized community support, explored alternative employee ownership plans, developed legislative agendas and engaged in direct action that included the occupation of Youngstown Sheet & Tube administration buildings and U.S. Steel headquarters in Pittsburgh.[22]

Russo and Linkon continue in their assessment of the work of the coalition: "In part because of the coalition's efforts, Congress eventually passed plant closing legislation to ensure workers adequate warnings of shutdowns. In other communities throughout the Rust Belt, local government organizations, guided by the Youngstown example, enlisted the principle of eminent domain, the right of the local community to claim ownership of private property for community uses, to claim abandoned industrial sites for a variety of community and economic development projects."[23]

Help from Jimmy Carter?

Let us return to the story of the Lykes-LTV merger. On 13 December 1979, the *Warren Tribune-Chronicle* pointed out that President Jimmy Carter's attorney general, Griffin Bell, had approved the Lykes-LTV merger over the objections of his staff, whom he termed "a bunch of messianics." The attorney general had added helpfully that "respectable businessmen do not shade facts." However, the workers saw matters differently. In an article entitled "Merger Approval Threatens

Shutdown," in the June-July 1978 issue of the *Brier Hill Unionist,* editor Gerald Dickey stated that Bell had invoked "the failing company doctrine" in approving the merger. Dickey also stated that the Brier Hill workers were at risk.[24] He was right.

In late October 1978, the Jones and Laughlin Steel Company (J & L), the subsidiary of LTV that owned the Brier Hill Works, first revealed plans to close the Brier Hill mill. This plan was announced publicly by the *Cleveland Plain Dealer* on 28 July 1979.[25] Now rank-and-file activists Ed Mann, John Barbero, Gerald Dickey, and others would be fighting not against the shutdown of someone else's mill but against the closing of the mill that was the source of their own jobs and those of their coworkers.

One significant difference between the closure of the Campbell Works and that of Brier Hill was that the Brier Hill local (USWA 1462) was run by militant rank-and-file activists. Workers like Ed Mann and John Barbero had been active in opposing the Steelworker's Experimental Negotiating Agreement in 1973. Moreover, their presence in Youngstown was one reason that Staughton and Alice Lynd decided to move to the city to begin their practice of law. Both Mann and Barbero believed that the heart and soul of a genuine labor movement were militantly democratic local unions with a strong system of shop stewards. These two men were strongly opposed to business unionism and in favor of union democracy and direct action when necessary.

Certain things seemed clear to those who led the fight by USWA Local 1462 against the closing of Brier Hill. First, as the struggle against the closing of the Campbell Works had demonstrated, Brier Hill workers were not likely to get much support or help from the international union, even though they paid dues to it and it was located only seventy-five miles away in Pittsburgh. President McBride and his leadership team took positions that betrayed their lack of concern for the plight of workers and their families; not only had McBride told union members from the Campbell Works in 1977 that the closing of a mill was like "the closing of the corner grocery store," but he had led the walkout from a Youngstown meeting on the feasibility of a worker- and community-owned mill. In fact, McBride seemed downright hostile to the independent plans of the Ecumenical Coalition because it was a grassroots movement that he could not control. McBride also consistently framed the issue of mill closures in terms of imported Japanese steel and the need for import quotas. This position by a labor leader must have delighted the executives at Lykes, because it let them off the hook for their own decision to close the mills. Second, local activists were clear about the complete lack of support they would get from the Carter Administration. Despite strong union support for Carter in the 1976 presidential election, his administration seemed deaf to the plight of Youngstown workers. Carter had won the 1976 election against then-President Gerald Ford by a very narrow margin in an Electoral College vote of 295 to 242. The AFL-CIO's Committee on Political Education (COPE), as well as international unions like the USWA, had poured money and volunteers into the task of electing Jimmy Carter. Yet less than one full year into Carter's term, his administration did virtually nothing to help Mahoning Valley steelworkers facing plant closings. Petitions and letters appealing to the president did no good. Petitioning steelworkers who had supported Carter with their votes were turned away at the gates of the White House. In addition, President Carter's attorney general, over the objections of his own staff, had approved the LTV-Lykes merger.

The Union vs. the Workers

Recognizing the futility of appealing for outside help, local leaders like Ed Mann, John Barbero, and Gerald Dickey turned to those values and tactics in which they believed: union democracy and solidarity. At least this time the local steelworkers and their supporters were not completely blindsided: many, such as Gerald Dickey, could see this closure coming as a result of the merger of LTV Steel and the Lykes Corporation. Ed Mann, John Barbero and other Local 1462 activists sought meetings with representatives of the Jones and Laughlin Steel Company regarding Brier Hill's closing. Staughton Lynd related that the international union attempted to shape the meetings between the local union and J & L by controlling who could be present. In the fall and winter of 1978, the international union excluded whomever it wished from the meetings between J & L and local and district union officials, even if the excluded individuals had been chosen by the local workers. Specifically, Frank Leseganich, then director of District 26 of the USWA, worked to exclude from the meetings community representatives such as Staughton Lynd, local clergy, and others who had belonged to the Ecumenical Coalition.[26]

Fearing anything resembling a public meeting on the mill closing, both the international union and J & L took the position that meetings between labor and management should be limited to those who are the legal "parties to the agreement" and should not include members of the wider community or their supporters. Lynd had been working with Local 1462 leaders on several concerns, including the filing of an unfair labor practice (ULP) against the company under the National Labor Relations Act. In this matter as well, the international union refused to support the efforts of the local union. Specifically, the international union declared that since the collective bargaining agreement was between it and the company, the local union could not be a party to the filing of a ULP without the international union's participation. The international union did not wish to file a ULP or to undertake any further litigation on the matter of the plant closing at Brier Hill. This marked the end of efforts by the leaders of Brier Hill Local 1462 and its community supporter to try to win through the established channels of the collective bargaining agreement and through federal labor law.[27]

From the winter of 1978 into the spring of 1979, Local 1462 and its community supporters launched a series of direct-action efforts to publicize the planned closing of Brier Hill and to put pressure on J & L Steel. These efforts included picketing and marches. On 19 January 1979, workers and community supporters picketed outside the Mahoning Valley Country Club where Youngstown Sheet & Tube superintendent Gordon Allen was speaking. On 17 March 1979, Local 1462 leaders, workers, and community supporters planned a downtown rally and march in Youngstown. The turnout was disappointing (about five hundred people) and seemed to point to a final and decisive defeat for those who had struggled so heroically to keep the mill open. Also in March, the Ecumenical Coalition received news that the Department of Commerce had turned down its request for the $100 million in loan guarantees necessary to reopen the Campbell works under worker and community ownership, a decision that marked the beginning of the end for the EC.

Defeat

At the end of March 1979, J & L made a final offer on Brier Hill to the workers at Local 1642. Staughton Lynd maintains that Frank Valenta, who had replaced Frank Leseganich as director of District 26 of the USWA, claimed that the international union was responsible for the "concessions" contained in J & L's final offer. However, when the international union met with company officials on 30 March 1979, the J & L letter to the Local 1462 membership was already in the mail. The company's offer contained many points, but these were the most important:

1. The Brier Hill Works would close.
2. The mill would most probably close on or around the end of 1979.
3. The company would not declare the mill closed until six months after the end of steelmaking at the mill.[28]

When the offer was put to a vote, it was carried by a margin of just under 2 to 1. The struggle at Brier Hill had come to an end. The valiant efforts of the local union leaders to keep the mill open had failed, and the mill did close at the end of December 1979.[29]

In the years following the struggle over the shutdown of Youngstown's steel mills, some of the principle actors passed on. Steelworkers president Lloyd McBride did not long survive Youngstown's steel crisis, for example, dying in 1983 at the age of sixty-seven. Staughton and Alice Lynd, together with all those who had fought to prevent the closure of the Brier Hill mill, were hit hard by the death of John Barbero, who was killed in 1981 in a fall from a ladder at his home. Twelve years later, in 1993, the Lynds would lose Ed Mann. His daughter Beth Hepfner, recalled that the Lynds had been more than collaborators with her father, being also good friends with both her parents. She greatly admired her father and remembered attending rallies and marches with a baby in tow as her dad spoke to workers. She mentioned that Staughton would always be close by, usually accompanied by Alice.[30]

With the Campbell Works closed by Youngstown Sheet & Tube and the Brier Hill Works closed by Jones and Laughlin, we now turn our attention to the surviving steel mills and their fate. In interviews, both Alice and Staughton Lynd often voiced their admiration of the many local steelworkers who turned out to oppose the closing of the mills, even when not directly affected. When Youngstown Sheet & Tube announced the closing of the Campbell Works in 1977, for example, workers like Ed Mann, John Barbero, and Gerald Dickey rushed to the aid of the mill's workers even though they worked at Brier Hill, which was still open.

Brownfield versus Greenfield

Now, in May 1979, with the Campbell Works closed and the Brier Hill Works slated for closure, the field of struggle moved to the remaining open mills, such as the Youngstown Works owned by U.S. Steel. The Youngstown Works contained two sites: the Ohio Works in Youngstown and the nearby McDonald Works in McDonald, Ohio. For these two mills, as for the Campbell and Brier Hill mills, the main issue was modernization. The burning question was, would the company spend the money necessary to modernize these two mills? The companies owning the Campbell and Brier Hill mills had decided not to modernize the existing facilities—an investment called brownfield development—instead choosing the relocate the steelmaking enterprise in the first case—greenfield development—and to simply close the mill and cease making steel altogether in the second case.

Staughton and Alice wrote the following about these two approaches to urban/industrial renewal:

> One evening after moving to Ohio, Staughton visited our friend John Barbero, a steelworker who lived near us in Niles. John showed Staughton a newspaper article in which Arizona politician Stewart Udall drew a contrast between "greenfield" and "brownfield" development. "Greenfield" development was what Robert Moses had proposed in Cooper Square [New York City]. You destroyed or walked away from an existing situation, and built something completely new from the ground up. This was also what U.S. Steel wanted to do with its steel mills. According to plans developed in the late 1970s, U.S. Steel would abandon its existing facilities in Youngstown and build an entirely new, state-of-the-art complex on the shore of Lake Erie in Conneaut, Ohio. The new mill would have polluted Lake Erie, destroyed a stopover refuge for migrating birds and endangered the vineyards that line the shore of the lake from Conneaut to Buffalo.[31]

The Lynds follow with a contrasting view of brownfield development: "'Brownfield' development, in contrast, was industrial renovation in the spirit of the Cooper Square Alternative Plan. You began with your existing assets. They were skilled workers, generations of whom had graduated from high school, perhaps spending a few years in military service, and then, with the help of an uncle, a father, or a brother, gone to work in the mill. There was an 'infrastructure' in the form of access roads and rail spurs. The question was how to preserve these existing assets while replacing the outdated steelmaking technology of the mills."[32]

However, brownfield development presented its own set of problems for cities like Youngstown. In the words of Sherry Linkon and John Russo of Youngstown State University:

> But brownfield redevelopment proved problematic. Over time, many of the mill structures were demolished and the landscape transformed into long meadows that belied what had existed and what remained in the ground. The Mahoning River and mill areas adjacent to it were found to be environmentally unsafe as a result of over one hundred years of largely unregulated iron and steelmaking and the dumping of industrial pollutants. According to the American Youth Hostel canoeing guide for the area, the Mahoning River 'is one of the most polluted streams in the U.S. and no one is trying to clean it up.' The cost of cleaning the brownfield sites was prohibitive because disturbing the polluted soil would stir up the toxins and there is no place to dump the polluted soil and sediment.[33]

USWA, Local 1330 v. U.S. Steel Corporation

Individual steelworkers and their supporters pointed to a number of promises made by company officials to keep the mill open if steelmaking could be made profitable in Youngstown. Staughton was working for Northeast Ohio Legal Services in the fall of 1979 when he and others filed a lawsuit against U.S. Steel (*USWA, Local 1330 v. U.S. Steel Corporation*) claiming that when one party (the company) makes a promise and another party (the workers at the mills) come to rely on this promise, an enforceable contract exists. Critics claimed that the management rights section of the Basic Steel Contract and the Experimental Negotiating Agreement between the USWA and U.S. Steel gave the company the sole discretionary right to close any of its mills as it saw fit. Staughton responded that the oral promises made by company officials created an additional contract (besides the written labor agreement) and that the company was bound to honor this additional contract as long as the mills remained profitable.[34] Moreover, Staughton argued that company promises to keep the mill open had prompted the workers at the mill to agree to concessions that helped to make the mill profitable, yet the company had decided unilaterally to close the mill anyway.[35]

After the suit had been filed in federal court and a trial date set, U.S. Steel announced that it would definitely close its two mills in March 1980, a decision that would result in the loss of between 5,000 and 6,000 jobs. As attorneys for the plaintiffs in the suit, Staughton and James Callen, the assistant director of Northeast Ohio Legal Services, sought an injunction to keep the mills open at least until after the trial. Recalling the period, James Callen noted that the case marked his first experience of working with Staughton on a case. He remarked that Staughton was meticulous, soft-spoken, eloquent, and well-prepared. Staughton handled the overall direction of the plaintiff's case, while Callen handled the direct examination of local steelworkers during the trial. During the closing arguments, Callen felt that Staughton did an incredible job of tying all elements of the plaintiff's case together.[36]

To return to the trial, in court Judge Thomas Lambros granted the injunction sought by the plaintiffs. Then, in an unexpected development, the judge spoke of the impact of the mill closings on workers and their families and on the larger community. Judge Lambros went on to suggest the possibility of some kind of local community right to industrial property, based on a long-established relationship between the local mills on the one hand and the workers and the community on the other.[37] The judge's remarks raised the hopes of the plaintiffs. As the trial concluded, however, Lambros ruled against the plaintiffs on both the "implied contract" argument and the "community right to industrial property" argument. The latter was particularly upsetting to the Staughton Lynd and the plaintiffs because it meant that the judge had ruled against a suit based in part on an argument that the judge himself had earlier suggested. Recalling that Judge Lambros read his decision, which was more than forty pages in length, Callen remarked that Lambros had clearly written his decision before he had heard the closing arguments presented by either side.[38]

With this disappointing decision, the struggle to prevent the closing of the steel mills of Youngstown and the greater Mahoning Valley ended. Beginning on "Black Monday," 19 September 1977, the workers and the larger community had fought the steel companies and the international

Workers protested the actions of U.S. Steel in 1980 by picketing. Kent State University Libraries. Special Collections and Archives.

This image was taken in 1980 during the U.S. Steel takeover. Kent State University Libraries. Special Collections and Archives.

union, using tools as varied as petition drives, demonstrations, building occupations, lobbying, and most creatively, the proposal of worker- and community-owned steel mills. This idea was not original, of course, but the Youngstown struggle gave it a new level of visibility.[39] If there is one single contribution that the Youngstown effort to save the steel mills open made to future struggles, it was its concentration, not on the traditional goal—usually promoted by local churches—of providing human services to unemployed steelworkers and their families (as important as that might be), but rather on the issue of the reemployment of those workers in jobs similar to those they had held before the shutdown of the mills. Simply put, the Ecumenical Coalition and both its religious and secular supporters (such as the Lynds) emphasized not welfare but meaningful work for those displaced by the shutdowns.

When Alice and Staughton moved from Chicago to the Youngstown area in 1976, they had already made contact with workers, who provided Staughton with a new perspective on the labor movement. Workers like Marty Glaberman, with his pamphlet *Punching Out*; rank-and-file activists like Ed Mann, John Barbero, and Bill Litch, with their opposition to the 1973 Steelworker Experimental Negotiating Agreement; workers like Stan Weir, with his ideas about the "informal work group" on the shop floor; and workers like John Sargent, with his experience of steelworker militancy predating the CIO, all helped to reorient Staughton in a direction consistent with the accompaniment values that he and Alice had tried to live and to apply. The steel mill closings, together with the complete lack of militancy, energy, or fortitude displayed by the Steelworker president Lloyd McBride and those around him, pushed Staughton even further in a new direction as he explored new forms of trade union organization. In this exploration, he would develop the concept of solidarity unionism and also work to build, with his close friends and comrades like Mann and Barbero, an alternative grouping of workers called the Workers Solidarity Club. Also out of his experiences with the steel mill closings came his book, *The Fight Against Shutdowns: Youngstown's Steel Mill Closings*, published by Stan Weir's small publishing house, Singlejack Books, in 1982. All of these experiences and influences helped determine the next chapter in the life of Staughton and Alice Lynd.

Chapter Seven ⟋⟍

SOLIDARITY UNIONISM

"For the union makes us strong."

RALPH CHAPLIN, IWW

Another Kind of Trade Unionism?

In 1992, the Charles H. Kerr Company published *Solidarity Union-ism: Rebuilding the Labor Movement from Below,* by Staughton Lynd. The book appeared about twenty years after Alice and Staughton Lynd conducted their interviews with rank-and-file workers in northern Indiana and Chicago. The experiences narrated by some of these men and women had changed Staughton's view of unions. By the 1990s, those changes had been augmented by many other experiences and observations: Alice's varied work experiences at Roosevelt University, for the Amalgamated Clothing Workers of America, as a paralegal for a small law firms; and after 1985 as an attorney with Northeast Ohio Legal Services; Staughton's experience of working for a law firm representing some of Youngstown's largest and most powerful unions, and Staughton's experiences and observations of unions, workers, and their community during the Youngstown steel closures of 1977–80. All these things prompted further evolution of the Lynds' views of unions.

Perhaps the single most influential event in helping Staughton to develop what he termed "solidarity unionism" was the Youngstown steel crisis of 1977–80.[1] Why? The negative example of the role of the international union in this crisis impelled the Lynds to seek newer and more responsive forms of unions and worker representation. The USWA's initial opposition to the plans of the local unions and the Ecu-menical Coalition to save local mills through worker and community ownership, together with its suspicion and hostility toward Staughton Lynd, at least partly because of his support of rank-and-file steelworkers opposed to the ENA, caused the Lynds to conclude that the international union was committed to a different kind of trade unionism. Although the USWA finally changed course and began to support employee stock ownership plans, and, much later, the worker-owned Mondragon cooperative in Spain, this shift occurred too late to save Youngstown's steel mills.

USWA leaders regarded their job as providing workers with good wages and benefits and then, if necessary, temporary financial support after a mill closed. They were taken aback by local steelworkers from the Youngstown region who demanded "jobs not welfare."[2] The USWA leaders felt they had done their job and that it was not their place to "tell the company how to run its business," as Lloyd McBride put it. To rank-and-file activists like Ed Mann and John Barbero, the USWA was a "top-down" union that didn't allow workers at the plant level even to vote on contracts. To Staughton, long committed to values of participatory democracy, self-organization, and horizontal working relationships, the USWA's attitude stimulated him to envision and write about an alternative form of unionism, one inspired in part by many local organizing efforts by workers in the 1930s, before the CIO came on the scene.[3] He was also influenced by Catholic liberation theology as practiced in Central America and by the example of the murdered Archbishop Oscar Romero of El Salvador. The considerable influence of Romero's life and ideas on both Alice and Staughton is demonstrated by their involvement in a series of discussions on his ideas, led by Staughton in the fall of 2011 at the Catholic Worker House in Youngstown.[4]

Business Unionism

One of Staughton's more recent collaborators is Andrej Grubacic, an anarchist originally from Yugoslavia who is also a historian and sociologist.[5] In his introduction to a 2010 collection of Staughton's essays and articles, Grubacic identifies three themes that characterize Staughton's political worldview: self-activity of workers and the poor; the importance of local communities and institutions; and solidarity.[6] Before exploring each of these elements, we will examine Staughton's view of the existing labor movement.

On many occasions, both in interviews and in his writings, Staughton has voiced pessimism (perhaps realism) about the potential of "reform" slates within particular unions to achieve any lasting fundamental change in either the structure or the mission of the labor movement:

> An easy way to remember the basic idea of solidarity unionism is to think: Horizontal not vertical. Mainstream trade unionism beyond the arena of the local union is relentlessly vertical. Too often, rank-and-file candidates for local union office imagine that the obvious next step for them is to seek higher office, as international union staff man, regional director, even international union president. The Left, for the past seventy-five years, has lent itself to the fantasy that salvation will come from above by the election of a John L. Lewis, Philip Murray, Walter Reuther, Arnold Miller, Ed Sadlowski, Ron Carey, John Sweeney, Andrew Stern, or Richard Trumka.[7]

Staughton Lynd and others, like his late comrades Stan Weir and Marty Glaberman, saw the existing trade union structure as characterized by workplace contractualism, the exclusive right of a single union to represent the workers in a given worksite, and waiver of the right to strike.

Workplace contractualism was institutionalized in many of the CIO unions that were born out of the worker's revolt of the 1930s. The most significant provisions of the new collective bargaining agreement were a "management rights" section, which took away many decisions formerly made by workers on the shop floor decisions and gave them to management, and a grievance procedure, which channeled and eventually bureaucratized workers' concerns over basic issues such as safety.

The policy of exclusive representation means that if one union, wins a representation election, even if it has the support of a bare majority of workers in a plant or office, that union becomes the exclusive representative of all the workers. This system is in keeping with the American notion of "winner take all" that is found at so many levels of our electoral process, but other systems do exist. In some European countries, minority unions are also accorded representation rights and then two or several unions form a coalition in order to bargain with the employer. Exclusive representation reduces the union's accountability to its members or to those in the bargaining unit who are not members. Another feature of the exclusive representation system is dues check-off, in which the employer deducts dues from the paycheck of the worker. This deduction is automatic and impersonal, and likewise serves to reduce the union's sense of accountability to its members. When some of the early industrial unions were formed, the shop steward went to each worker and collected dues. While some may say that this system was onerous and old-fashioned, the fact remains that it did bring home to union leaders their direct accountability to the membership. Increasingly, with exclusive representation and dues check-off, union leaders come to regard the worker as an inconvenience, to be listened to only when it cannot be avoided. Staughton has come to the conclusion that "reforms" such as exclusive representation and dues check-off have had the unintended negative consequence of distancing the union leadership from the rank and file.

One of the developments most damaging to the power of workers on the shop floor was the signing by the CIO unions of collective bargaining agreements that included no-strike clauses over the life of the contract. Only after a contract expired could workers again exercise their right to withdraw their services. We have seen how some business unionists such as Steelworker president I. W. Abel, agreed in the Experimental Negotiating Agreement to waive the right to strike altogether. Stan Weir, in his contribution to Alice and Staughton's first collection of interviews, *Rank and File*, talks about the "informal work group" on the shop floor as the key to building workers' power from the bottom up. Basing this concept on his experience as a seaman, Weir contended that the work group on the shop floor was the worker's immediate community. Such work groups, through local decision-making, could solve problems and deal with management in a timely manner, or go on strike if necessary. Weir argued that this is the most effective way to humanize this workplace.[8] Weir complains that the business unionism practiced by modern international unions seeks merely to win such benefits as early retirement. The union thus delivers benefits to workers but ignores the issue of worker power on the shop floor.[9]

Solidarity Unionism

From these criticisms of contemporary business unionism, Staughton developed an alternative vision, which he and others call solidarity unionism. Staughton's vision of solidarity unionism is based on strong feelings about the subject:

> I have gone at it as a historian, as a practicing lawyer, as a reader to the best of my ability in the Marxist classics and there is nothing about which I feel more passionately than this idea. There is a positive outcome, mainly a model of a kind of unionism which my friends and I call Solidarity Unionism, in which I very much believe. Nothing is more attractive or inspiring or hopeful about the labor movement than the idea of solidarity. The concept that an injury to one is an injury to all. I began to feel that the way the whole machinery of trade unionism and labor law had come to work in the United States did not encourage solidarity.[10]

In examining this new vision, it is useful to return to Andrej Grubacic's attempt to "organize" Staughton's vision around three principles: self-activity of workers and the poor; the importance of local communities and institutions; and solidarity.[11]

The fundamental principle of self-activity has two important aspects. The first is the idea that we don't need a huge "international" union (which is actually national with a couple of locals in Canada) with a top-down command structure, seeking to compete with other unions with nearly identical mindsets, to organize the workers in a given industry or factory. Such international unions practice vertical unionism, with decisions being made in Washington, D.C., or wherever the union headquarters happen to be. The leadership and national staff of such unions have all the trappings of a corporation, and they use power as a conduit to keep decisions flowing from the top down.

A good, recent example of a union with such a structure and mindset is the Service Employees International Union (SEIU) under the leadership of Andrew Stern. Dissident locals were placed in trusteeship, or "reorganized," in order to eliminate centers of opposition or even independent thinking. But what happens if the local membership objects to having the local that they organized taken over by SEIU staff from Washington? Simple! In his book, *Labor's Civil Wars in California*, Cal Winslow related the story of a SEIU Washington, D.C., staff person, telling healthcare workers whose local had just been taken over by national SEIU staff that if they didn't disperse, she would call the police on them—so much for solidarity and union democracy. As an alternative to the model just described, Staughton Lynd asks us to look to different models, such as the unions preceding CIO unions in cities like Minneapolis and Toledo. These unions reached out, not vertically but horizontally, to form alliances with other local unions, thus creating a kind of informal network. Such alliances might include locals of the same union or locals of different unions that see an advantage in cooperating.[12]

In his essay, "From Globalization to Resistance," Staughton drew inspiration from Russian soviets, Italian factory committees, and some unions in the United States that put local organizing and workplace democracy ahead of national drives for power and control.[13]

Another aspect of the concept of self-activity by working people is demonstrated by the way the Zapatistas revolted in the state of Chiapas, in extreme southern Mexico near the border with Guatemala, in 1994, the year after the North American Free Trade Act (NAFTA) was passed by Congress and signed by President Clinton. The two events stood in sharp contrast. One was an effort to extend the "free" market in such a way as to bring Mexico even more under the hegemony of American capitalism. The other was a local act not so much of protest as of organized defiance. Staughton applauds the Zapatistas for working not to seize power but to build networks in and among communities in Chiapas. He sees the work of the Zapatistas as a contemporary example of (to paraphrase a line from the constitution of the IWW) building a new society within the shell of the old.[14]

The importance of local communities and institutions, the second principle identified by Grubacic as a pillar of Staughton's imagined house of labor, is closely related to self-activity. However, it embodies the positive hope that through the spontaneous actions of workers, new local institutions, along the lines of like E. P. Thompson's "warrens," can be created. In the introduction to his edited collection of Staughton's essays, Andrej Grubacic writes, "But what is Thompson's warren? And why do I insist that it represents a formula for success? It is, first and foremost, a local institution in which people conduct their own affairs—an immigrant center or local union, for example— that expands in time of crisis to take on new powers and responsibilities, and then, after the revolutionary tide ebbs, continues to represent, in institutionalized form, an expanded version of what existed to begin with."[15] Since the local self-activity in zones of struggle like Chiapas is continually creative, older institutions, like churches or local *campesino* cooperatives, exist alongside new local structures, like self-defense organizations, as the transformation takes place gradually over time. These formations take on new duties and are vested with new moral authority by those who created them.

The third principle informing the new kind of union envisioned by Staughton, according to Grubacic, is solidarity. While there are different kinds of solidarity, Staughton has written in particular about the idea of accompaniment. Accompaniment encompasses one of the most dramatic demonstrations of solidarity. It requires the "organizer" to step over the line that separates him or her from the workers or small farmers or rural poor who are oppressed. Accompaniment requires that when an organizer comes to the neighborhood or village, he or she comes to stay. The organizer walks with the oppressed in their struggles, lives in their neighborhoods, befriends them, and learns from them as they learn from him or her. The organizer should have a specific skill or skills (e.g., those of a teacher, a lawyer, or perhaps even a clergy member) to offer to the poor or the workers who are in struggle. The organizer does not come to those in struggle in order to preach to them but to live with them in community and in shared struggle.

Many left-wing sects promote a kind of vanguardist approach to working with the oppressed. They believe, based on an application of some of Lenin's writings, that workers and the poor, if left to their own devices, will never rise to the appropriate level of revolutionary consciousness without some "education" by the professional revolutionary. The professional revolutionary is with—but not part of—the local community. Because such an activist has "valuable" theoretical understanding, he or she cannot be spared to work in a particular community if the result does not look promising. The goal of helping the workers or the poor in need, while professed to be important, is always seen as secondary to the task of promoting and growing the revolutionary party.

It was inevitable that the values associated with accompaniment would lead Alice and Staughton to embrace the cause of workers and yet reject the existing structure and philosophy of trade unionism prevalent in the United States today. Just as Silone's tragic hero, Pietro Spina, would embrace the values of socialism and yet reject the structure and values of the Italian Communist Party, Alice and Staughton, through their own experiences, have done the same with trade unionism: supporting workers and their families while rejecting business unionism. In envisioning a new model of unionism, Staughton identifies several elements that it should embrace. First, self-activity from below is critical. The strength and power must come from the local unions through shop-floor militancy and strike action. In such a model, different unions in the same plant must reach over jurisdictional lines and work together. Finally, in the best spirit of accompaniment, the local leaders must be of the workers and identify with their needs and concerns. The local leadership must "walk with," or accompany, the workers in their struggles.

From here we turn to an examination of some alternatives to business unionism with which Staughton and Alice have been associated: those featuring self-organization, local institutions, and solidarity, the key principles underlying what has come to be called solidarity unionism.

Chapter Eight

SPECIFIC ALTERNATIVES TO BUSINESS UNIONISM

"I think we've got too much contract."

ED MANN

In his writings on solidarity unionism, Staughton often cites examples of what solidarity unionism in the United States might look like. These examples are not prescriptive; Staughton believes that solidarity unionism can take many different forms. The key element is simply the horizontal, nonhierarchical relationships both among members within an organization and between workers belonging to several different organizations. The Lynds have been involved with four groups whose work embodied solidarity unionism: the Workers Solidarity Club; Solidarity USA; Workers Against Toxic Chemical Hazards (WATCH); and Visiting Nurses.

Workers Solidarity Club

When the Lynds moved from Chicago to Youngstown in 1976 to begin the practice of law, Staughton hoped, naïvely, that his activist past would not become an issue too soon as he and Alice sought to establish a new life for themselves and their family. However, such hopes are rarely fulfilled as we expect. In 1976, the *Youngstown Vindicator* carried a 1965 photo featuring Staughton, Dave Dellinger, and Bob Moses protesting the war in Vietnam in a march sponsored by the Assembly of Unrepresented People. All three men had been splattered by red paint (symbolizing blood) thrown on them by counterdemonstrators who favored the war. The impact of this photo's republication in Youngstown,

Bob Schindler contacted Staughton on behalf of his brother-in-law, Jack ("Union Jack") Walsh, after Walsh saw a famous photograph in the *Youngstown Vindicator* of Staughton and fellow antiwar demonstrators Dave Dellinger and Bob Moses covered in blood at a rally. When he saw the photograph, Walsh declared, "That's the lawyer for me!" Kent State University Libraries. Special Collections and Archives.

eleven years after it was taken, was perhaps exactly the opposite of the one Staughton had feared. Soon after, Staughton received a phone call from Jack Walsh, known as "Union Jack" and the brother-in-law of Bob Schindler. Walsh had just been fired by the Schwebel Baking Company for leading an "unauthorized" strike. When he saw the photo in the *Vindicator,* he said: "Now that's the lawyer for me!"[1] Schindler asked Staughton if he would lead a series of classes on labor law to help workers understand their rights under existing labor law. Staughton said he would, and he did. The classes were held in the hall of Utility Workers Local 118 in Youngstown.

From these classes evolved the Workers' Solidarity Club. In his book *Solidarity Unionism,* Staughton quoted several club members explaining the reasons the club came into existence. One worker commented: "We wanted a place where rank-and-file-workers could go to get strike support without a lot of hassle and delay. We were disillusioned with big national unions that encourage their members to 'pay your dues and leave the rest to us.'"[2] Another participant remembers the following: "We were called 'rebels' and 'dissidents' but we believed in solidarity, and we wanted a way to see each other regularly, share experiences, laugh at each other's jokes, and dream up plans to change the world."[3] Staughton describes the club as follows:

> From the beginning, the Club has been extremely informal. There are no officers except a treasurer. Two members get out a monthly notice describing what is expected to happen at the next meeting. Individuals volunteer (or are volunteered at the last moment) to chair particular meetings. If there is a speaker at a particular meeting, the person who invited the speaker is likely to become chairperson. There are no dues, but by passing the hat we have raised hundreds of dollars for legal defense, publications, and travel expenses. We also raise money by selling bright red suspenders with the words 'Workers' Solidarity' silk-screened in black. Beer at the end of every meeting, and annual picnics and Christmas parties, keep us cheerful.[4]

The club provided support for a strike by AFSCME workers at Trumbull Memorial Hospital in 1982, and it conducted classes for union activists. Members of the Workers Solidarity Club even edited a newsletter, *Impact*, which addressed not only labor subjects but also issues such as prisoner rights. While many works and prisoners contributed to the

Staughton was a familiar sight on the picket line in this April 1996 photograph. Kent State University Libraries. Special Collections and Archives.

Staughton was a founder of the Workers' Solidarity Club in 1981. Pictured here at a local rally, Staughton is on the right holding the banner. Kent State University Libraries. Special Collections and Archives.

Ed Mann, wearing a cap and holding a bullhorn, and Staughton, on the extreme left in a stocking cap knitted by his son Lee Lynd, prepare for a Worker's Solidarity Club rally. Kent State University Libraries. Special Collections and Archives.

Members of the Workers' Solidarity Club and others march down a road to picket. Kent State University Libraries. Special Collections and Archives.

newsletter, which was published monthly for more than fifteen years, the tone and focus of the publication reflected Staughton's voice.

Solidarity USA

In 1985, Alice graduated from the University of Pittsburgh Law School and joined Staughton as an attorney at Northeast Ohio Legal Services. Not long after that, LTV Steel, the corporation that had acquired three steel companies (Youngstown Sheet & Tube, Republic, and Jones and Laughlin) declared bankruptcy and promptly ceased paying retiree medical benefits. This new struggle for the benefits of retired steelworkers was the first time that Staughton and Alice worked together *as lawyers* on the same struggle.

Writing in *Stepping Stones*, Alice and Staughton described how a working woman created the impetus that led to the formation of Solidarity USA and to the struggle by retired steelworkers and their families to recover the benefits that LTV had taken away from them:

Delores Hrycyk (pronounced "her-is-sik"), wife of an LTV Steel retiree, worked as a receptionist in the office of an optometrist two floors below our Legal Services office. Mrs. Hrycyk telephoned Youngstown-area radio stations and called a meeting of LTV Steel retirees to be held in the public square the next Saturday. A thousand people attended. Mrs. Hrycyk invited those interested to attend a second meeting a few days later. On that occasion she asked, "What shall we call ourselves?" A man suggested from the floor that we resembled Polish Solidarity. All right, Delores responded, we'll call ourselves "Solidarity USA."[5]

While in law school, Alice had made a point of learning all she could about pension law because it was so much needed in Youngstown. Lawyers who knew pension law worked for companies, unions, the government, or universities. Very few lawyers had any experience advocating for workers who were losing their pensions or other employee or retiree benefits.

Alice and Staughton became the lawyers for Solidarity USA. In many unions, retirees do not vote on the sections of a new collective bargaining agreement that deal with their health and retirement benefits. Their attempts to obtain a voice inside the union are rarely welcomed by the union leadership. However, the members of Solidarity USA sought to overcome these problems by simply being present and asking to speak with company officials from LTV or the various insurance companies and with union leaders from the USWA. In order for elderly retirees to attend meetings and other actions, Solidarity USA chartered buses.

Alice and Staughton described the tactics of the retirees:

> Solidarity USA sought to overcome this handicap by its physical presence. Elderly men and women took long chartered bus rides to city council meetings in Cleveland and Pittsburgh, and to the headquarters in those cities of LTV Steel, Blue Shield/ Blue Cross, and the Steelworkers union; to Congressional hearings in Washington, D.C.; and to sessions of bankruptcy court in New York City. Our standard *modus operandi* was not to ask for a meeting but to inform the targeted party that we would arrive on a certain day. If they met with us, we said politely, well and good; if not, they could anticipate a very large picket line. Our uniform experience was that, after our chartered buses from Youngstown, Cleveland, Pittsburgh, Aliquippa, and Canton arrived, we would be invited inside. If the invitation was limited to a designated number of people or to "your leaders" or "your lawyers," we would make it clear that we had a committee that included a number of retirees who would describe their own experiences. We were never refused.[6]

There is little doubt that Solidarity USA was effective as an advocate organization for LTV Steel retirees. By the time the company finally emerged from bankruptcy, the retirees were able to regain most of the retirement benefits that LTV Steel had initially tried to take away from them. In the course of the retiree struggles to regain their benefits, Alice became especially adept at working with the retirees in sorting out what various pension or benefit plans provided.

Workers Against Toxic Chemical Hazards (WATCH)

In 1988, Alice and Staughton assisted a group of workers who had been chemically poisoned while on the job. The four autoworkers were from the General Motors plant at Lordstown, Ohio. They had been referred to Staughton by a local state legislator and met with the Lynds in the offices of Northeast Ohio Legal Services. There were problems in parts of the Lordstown plant. Fumes above the plant were sucked back into the building. Within the plant, fumes were recirculated. Fumes from different sources were allowed to mix together, making them more toxic. Employees spraying paint on newly assembled automobiles in the paint booth worked with inadequate protection. Alice and Staughton did not expect much in the way of assistance from General Motors. However, they also got no help from the UAW local in the plant. In fact, the union was hostile because the local leadership feared that if they caused too many problems for the company, the Lordstown plant might not get the next model car to produce, resulting in lost jobs or even in closure of the plant.[7]

Together with others, the four workers formed Workers Against Toxic Chemical Hazards. The workers had noticed the high number of former employees of GM's Lordstown plant who were dying younger than one would expect. The workers came up with the idea of going through the newspaper obituaries to confirm their suspicions. They did. In order to bring this information to the attention of the public, the workers decided to construct a memorial to the deceased Lordstown workers by putting their names and ages at time of death on large sheets of plywood to be shown to the public when they called a press conference. The press conference was held, drawing reporters from other cities, such as Akron and Cleveland. Workers chaired the press conference, and though representatives of both the company and the union came, they elected to leave early and to take no role. As a result of the press conference, General Motors and the UAW decided to support a PMR (proportional mortality ratio) study. When it was completed and the results were announced, the data showed that death rates for workers at the Lordstown plant were significantly higher than they were for the population as a whole. The death rate from pancreatic cancer among Lordstown workers was *seven times* higher than that of the general population.[8]

Visiting Nurses Association (VNA)

In another example of solidarity unionism, Alice and Staughton worked with nurses and home health aides employed by the Visiting Nurses Association of Youngstown. These busy and overworked health workers, who also had family commitments to tend to, came together to form Visiting Nurses Solidarity. In many of their other efforts at solidarity unionism, the Lynds assisted disabled workers, laid-off workers, or workers from different unions to organize around a specific issue or to create an alternative to the existing central labor bodies. In the case of the visiting nurses and home health aides, however, Alice and Staughton worked alongside people who were trying to form a union in what had been a nonunion shop. Gradually, as the nurses and other home health workers gained some experience and confidence in doing such important tasks as grievance representation and contract negotiations, the Lynds, as lawyers for Youngstown's VNA, stepped quietly into the background. In its early days, the new union at the VNA exhibited many of the less formal organizational norms championed by Staughton in his writings on solidarity unionism. For example, the nurses initially had no formal dues structure, instead simply "passing the hat" when they needed money. This lack of formal dues in turn meant that there was no need for dues check-off. Finally, the nurses in Visiting Nurses Solidarity interacted in ways similar to those proposed by Stan Weir for his model of the informal work group: they simply looked for each other and stood together in solidarity when such unity was required.

The first three of the four groups discussed above no longer exist; the VNA nurse's union does still exist, but it is now affiliated with SEIU. Nevertheless, it is important to view the existence and the work of all four groups as attempts by workers disenchanted with traditional unions to reach out to each other around common issues. These workers sought *new forms* of organization in order to continue their struggle to resolve issues that existing unions refused to address or that arose after workers retired or lost their jobs and thus became unrepresented. Organizations formed by workers do not always have to be permanent in order to serve the important goal of showing workers that other forms of organization are possible and that the workers can build such new groups themselves. Writing in *Solidarity Unionism,* Staughton summarized the key differences between traditional unions and the organizations described above in the following areas: membership, dues, paid staff, and legalism.[9]

Membership

Once a union has been recognized as the exclusive bargaining agent for workers in a given plant or worksite, belonging to that union is compulsory. For Ohio public employees, membership remains voluntary unless the public employer and the union agree to include in the collective bargaining agreement a provision called Agency Shop (or fair share). Under this provision, a public employee must either join the union or pay a service fee to the union to cover the cost to the union of representing the employee. For workers in the private sector, Ohio is one of twenty-five states that permit the union and the company to bargain and establish the union shop, a system permitted under the National Labor Relations Act of 1935 (NLRA). In 1947, the NLRA was amended by a law popularly known as the Taft-Hartley Act, which, in its infamous section 14-B, permits states to outlaw the union shop. Now, after recent victories in Indiana and Michigan, conservative, antiunion forces have managed to get the union shop provision of the NLRA outlawed in twenty-five of fifty states. Briefly stated, the union shop provision makes union membership a condition of employment. Usually, a newly hired worker has a period of time after date of hire (usually ninety days) to join the union. Thus, in cases where the collective bargaining agreement contains a union shop provision, union membership is compulsory after a specified period following the date of hire.

By contrast, in groups practicing solidarity unionism—groups like Solidarity USA, the Workers Solidarity Club, and Visiting Nurses Solidarity—membership is voluntary. In states (called "right-to-work" states) where the union shop cannot be bargained in a collective bargaining agreement, the union must regularly campaign among the workers to get the workers to renew their membership.

The Collection of Dues

In traditional unions dues check-off provisions are common. Such provisions permit an employer to deduct automatically from the worker's pay a monthly prorated portion of the dues. In many collective bargaining agreements, a dues check-off provision is considered a minor administrative detail.

Alice and Staughton see the matter differently. For them, the existence of regular dues and the way in which they are collected affect a local union's accountability to the workers it represents. When dues collection is automatic and is done by the company controller, the Lynds believe that a key element of union responsibility to the workers had been lost. On the other hand, when the shop steward must directly contact each worker to collect his or her dues, the steward comes face to face with the workers the union represents, underlining a sense of accountability. The Lynds' view of on this matter is diametrically opposed to that held by the leaders of traditional trade unions at all levels, as well as to that of their social democratic supporters. Thus, not surprisingly, solidarity organizations, like the four described which Alice and Staughton helped bring into existence, generally raise money through voluntary contributions collected on the spot for each particular action or expense item. By "passing the hat," these groups emphasize the democratic, collective nature of their organization.

Paid Union Staff

Except for very small locals, most traditional unions have one or more paid members of staff, who can develop interests distinct from those of the workers they are supposed to represent. Workers who rise to become local union presidents or business agents often find their priorities shifting. As their distance from the shop floor increases, they become concerned less with representing the interests of the local workers and more concerned with preserving their own positions by consolidating control and identifying potential rivals. They wish to retain the coveted paid staff jobs that raised them from the shop floor and gave them a larger salary—often many times larger than that a worker would make.

In contrast, groups practicing solidarity unionism, like the Youngstown area organizations discussed above, have no paid staff. Meeting chairs and other positions are voluntary and usually rotate.

Legalism

The legal focus of the traditional union is almost exclusively on the enforcement of the terms and conditions of the collective bargaining agreement between the union and the employer. If a problem arises, the worker is told to file a grievance and then stand back and let the paid staff resolve the matter. In addition, with what little authority he has left the shop steward often ends up (in the words of Marty Glaberman) being a "cop for the boss."[10]

Conversely, in groups practicing solidarity unionism (like those described above), specific grievances do not give place to the provisions of a collective bargaining agreement. Moreover, when a grievance arises, the members do not yield control over their response to a paid staff member. Instead, they employ a variety of tactics and actions to demonstrate the importance of an issue and obtain a resolution.

The Outside Organizer

Colin Bossen is a former IWW union organizer who served in Cleveland Heights, Ohio, as parish minister for the Unitarian Universalist Society of Cleveland. Bossen has left the pulpit and is now a graduate student in American history at Harvard University. In a journal article, Bossen wrote of his efforts to organize bike messengers and also touched on solidarity unionism, as advocated by Staughton Lynd. Bossen is a believer in many of the tenets of solidarity unionism, as articulated by Staughton Lynd and as based on some of the earlier ideas of both Weir and Glaberman.

The article, which appeared in *Working USA*, dealt with the efforts of Bossen and others to unionize bike messengers into the Chicago Couriers Union (CCU), affiliated with the IWW; Bossen served as a volunteer organizer in this effort for two years, from 2003 to 2005.[11] In his article, Bossen offers a sympathetic critique of solidarity unionism.[12]

Bossen reports the paradox that while the union of bike messengers might never have been formed without help from outside organizers from the IWW, differences of perspective soon arose between the organizers and the bike messengers. The existence of these differences retarded the development of local leaders from among the ranks of the bike messengers. Nevertheless, Bossen concludes, based on his and other's efforts to organize around the principles of solidarity unionism, that a paid outside organizer was essential for success in organizing the messengers. In responding to this conclusion, Staughton Lynd observes that bicycle messengers work alone and thus lack the opportunity for collective self-organization on the job available to most workers.

The role of the organizer is an issue that has divided the Left and labor intellectuals since the 1930s. In his monumental history of the United Farm Workers under Caesar Chavez, for example, Frank Bardacke outlines how Chavez was influenced by such organizers as Saul Alinsky and Fred Ross. Bardacke notes that Alinsky, in his book *Reveille for Radicals* (1946), depicts the organizer as a heroic figure who enjoys the "complete faith" of the people and suggests that the importance of this faith may sometimes embolden the organizer to mislead or manipulate the people to get them ready to struggle for the cause. In Bardacke's words:

> Alinsky's disdain for "moral quibbling" is perhaps responsible for his failure to consider in either work [*Reveille for Radicals* or the much later *Rules for Radicals* (1971)] one of the most elementary problems of the ends versus means debate: Is there any difference between the tactics that can be used among friends and the tactics that can be used against enemies? After Alinsky demonstrates how the organizer uses questionable techniques among friends to put the PO [People's Organization] together, he then shows how the organizer can use a whole arsenal of dirty tricks against the community's enemies. Do both sets of tricks come out of the same bag?[13]

When Mark Weber heard Alinsky speak at Colgate University in the winter of 1969, he remembers the speaker's reference to the "tender moral sensibilities" of the New Left. Bardacke refers to a similar comment by Alinsky and then states that *Rules for Radicals* was written a quarter of a century later in order to appeal to the moral sensibilities of the New Left. The reason for this small detour into the world of Saul Alinsky is to make the point that some on the left, remembering Alinsky's theory *and* practice concerning how outside organizers function, might be suspicious of outside organizers who function for the workers, but who are apart from them. As for Staughton, although he is not suspicious of all outside organizers, his knowledge of the Alinsky method and his experience in organizing in other settings causes him to share Bardacke's fundamental reservations about the Alinsky method.

Support from Labor Institutions

Bossen asserts that solidarity unionism undervalues the importance of institutional support. "The CCU was only able to succeed," he argues, "because of the institutional support it received. The larger IWW helped pay for organizers, provided the infrastructure in the form of the local Chicago GMB's [General Membership Branch] union hall and bank accounts, gave the union legal standing with the National Labor Relations Board (NLRB), connected the union with legal counsel, held organizer training, and even published flyers and distributed information about the union via the Chicago GMB's newsletter."[14] As a result of these observations, Bossen concludes that Staughton's efforts to outline solidarity unionism as an alternative to business unionism, admirable as they might be, create the impression among his many readers that unions appear spontaneously. To Bossen, writings by Lynd and the IWW organizer at Starbucks, Daniel Gross, tend to minimize the role of the organizer and to stress the spontaneity of trade union formation at the local shop or office level.[15]

In concluding his essay, Bossen notes that Lynd and Gross, in the updated edition of *Labor Law for the Rank and Filer,* have added a section on solidarity unionism. While they affirm in this section the central role of the rank and file, Bossen points out that they also acknowledge that outside organizations and individuals may have a role to play as long as the end result is the enhancement of rank and file control.[16] Bossen sees the importance of solidarity unionism being a "good fit" for worksites like bike messenger shops where a large number of employees are considered "independent contractors" or are divided by job, skill, or location. He feels that these kinds of industries encourage the existence of informal work groups in which solidarity unionism can take root and then grow horizontally.

Bossen's friendly critique of solidarity unionism comes from a Wobbly and an organizer strongly influenced by Staughton Lynd's ideas but who nevertheless believes that reliance on skilled outside organizers and outside union support is sometimes essential.[17] In the sense that solidarity unionism is a collection of values rather than a doctrine that must be applied on a "take it or leave it" basis, no doubt Staughton would agree.

In April 1998, Staughton Lynd gave an address to the Friends of the Kent State University Library entitled "Labor History, Oral History, and May 4th." After his address, he engaged in a friendly yet pointed exchange with Jean Tussey (1918–2010), a socialist and trade unionist who was one of the founders of the Greater Cleveland Labor History Society. Jean was active in the Ohio State Labor Party, which was the state affiliate of the Labor Party organized by Tony Mazzocchi (1926–2002) at a 1995 convention in Cleveland.[18] The point at issue between Tussey and Staughton was when to run candidates for office on a local labor party ticket. Not surprisingly, Staughton argued for the spontaneous decision of local groups to run candidates, while Tussey argued for a more disciplined and structured approach, in which the state affiliate would decide when and where local labor candidates could run based on whether or not a credible campaign could be mounted. Staughton consistently stood for a decentralized approach; Tussey, for internal discipline and centralized decision-making.

In this informal argument between two veteran radicals, one could see emerging the same themes present in earlier debates over the nature of the labor movement in which Staughton had engaged: local autonomy, self-activity, and reaching out to community groups. Staughton also objected to the manner in which the Labor Party had weighted voting, based on unions voting to affiliate with it. Staughton remained suspicious of trade union leaders playing the same role in the new Labor Party that they played in the Democratic Party. The argument between Jean Tussey and Staughton Lynd anticipated the general debate in some sections of the Labor Party about when to run candidates. Eventually, the Labor Party declined in strength but it still exists in some states, including Ohio.[19]

Business Unionism versus Social Unionism

A final dimension of the labor movement to which Staughton made an invaluable contribution was the analysis of business unionism relative to social unionism. The standard analysis contrasts the two, using George Meany (1894–1980) as the symbol of conservative business unionism and Walter Reuther (1907–1970) as the shining symbol of social unionism. Staughton critiqued this analysis, providing a new perspective.

Many see business unionism as focused almost exclusively on servicing the existing membership, administering the collective bargaining agreement with the boss, and developing support for local Democratic and Republican politicians. In contrast, people tend to see social unionism as seeking to organize workers as yet unorganized and supporting social causes such as civil rights and the struggles of farmworkers.

Staughton Lynd has challenged this dichotomy as simplistic. For example, he has spoken and written about the role that Walter Reuther played at the 1964 Democratic Convention in Atlantic City, New Jersey, working with Lyndon Johnson's operatives to deny seating to delegates from the Mississippi Freedom Democratic Party in favor of the lily-white delegation from the regular Democratic Party of Mississippi. This action alienated the young civil rights workers from Mississippi who had risked death to try to bring some measure of citizenship to the black citizens of the Magnolia State. By the 1960s and 1970s, many Americans saw Walter Reuther as the face of social unionism, yet in fact this meant little more than walking in somebody else's picket line or and standing with farmworkers.

According to Reuther's biographer, Nelson Lichtenstein, in his book *The Most Dangerous Man in Detroit* (1995), auto workers were, by the late 1960s, enduring speedups on the production line that provoked a new wave of worker militancy, most notably through the rise of the black-led revolutionary union movement. Inside the United Automobile Workers (UAW), however, the lieutenants of the Reuther machine seemed little inclined to take the kind of militant direct action that their predecessors had taken as young workers in the 1936 sit-down strikes, regarding revolutionary unionism with suspicion and alarm. In response, young black workers responded with scorn when UAW leaders failed to support them in resolving issues on the shop floor while

Reuther, their international union president, marched elsewhere, in support of other workers' picket lines.[20] It became clear to those who cared about such matters (like Staughton Lynd) that for all the marketing of the social unionism of this or that labor leader (Reuther in the 1960s, for example, and Andrew Stern in the 1990s), such public support for organizing did not translate into practical support on grassroots issues like internal union democracy.

In another of his books, *Labor's War at Home* (1982), Lichtenstein paints a generally unflattering picture of Reuther. He points out that in 1943, when his factional opponents within the UAW proposed breaking wildcat strikes and disciplining workers who violated the wartime no-strike pledge, Reuther opposed these harsh measures against workers. The following year, however, when similar wildcat strikes took place in Reuther's own Chevrolet Division and embarrassed him, he employed, without much hesitation, the very same heavy-handed tactics he had attacked the year before when advocated by his rivals within the union.[21]

Both the Reuther administration of the 1960s and the Stern administration of the 1990s were "one-party states," in which even simple dissenters voicing opposition to the leadership were consigned to the margins of the union. Frank Bardacke, in *Trampling Out the Vintage*, makes a similar analysis of the evolution of the United Farmworkers under Caesar Chavez. Bardacke argues that the gradual adoption of antidemocratic practices by the Chavez leadership contributed to the decline of the UFW.[22]

Staughton, both in interviews and in his writings, has expressed skepticism at the "reform" movements inside the existing unions. His critique of the existing labor movement is both ideological and structural. He asserts that a well-meaning reformer, like Ed Sadlowski of the Steelworkers Union, who ran for international president in 1976 against the establishment candidate, Lloyd McBride, would not have been able to fundamentally change the culture of the Steelworkers Union because he would simply have been placing his hands on the old top-down machinery of union governance and trying to wield it in a progressive fashion.[23] Inevitably, progressive, top-down reform will run against militant action by the rank and file, action that may have a local focus and reject the workplace contractualism that is at the heart of both business unionism and progressive social union reform.

The heart of solidarity unionism is not the negotiation of new labor agreements every three years or so, with no-strike clauses and long lists of management rights. Instead, its core is local participatory democracy and organization together with horizontal cooperation: elected shop floor committees that would organize and function around workplace demands rather than around desired clauses in a new labor agreement with the boss. This approach could function in a unionized plant as well as in a plant or worksite in which there was no union.

In *The Fall of the House of Labor* (1987), labor historian David Montgomery cites examples of workers in shops and factories during and after World War I who organized into shop floor committees that cut across craft lines and united all workers in the plant. These plant-level committees confronted the boss in places like Pittsburgh. What made them so effective? First, the shop floor committees had the trust of the local workers: they knew their committeemen. Second, the local committee knew the workplace issues and reflected the work culture of the shop. Third, the local committee members were *always* present, *every day*, to talk with workers and to stand up with them. These were strengths unavailable to a national union.[24]

Visionary Syndicalism versus Contractualism

In considering the two visions of worker organization presented above, it might be useful to explore one aspect of their practical application: the strategy necessary to provide long-term support for militant union locals opting for a kind of "visionary syndicalism" over the contractualism of conservative unions. Roy Worthman, in his book *From Syndicalism to Trade Unionism* (1985), makes the following observation about the efforts of IWW Industrial Union 440 to balance the IWW's commitment to revolutionary unionism with the demand by many in the rank and file for contracts that defined the relationship between the worker and the employer:

> IWW victories at Lawrence, Massachusetts, and the Mesabi iron range in Minnesota came to naught because the IWW constitution forbade time agreements (collective bargaining agreements for a fixed period of years) and thus forced a loss in membership. The same was true for

the 1927–1928 Columbine Coal Strike in Colorado, when the IWW lost membership to the UMW due to the contract issue. Given this background, and the fact that the IWW membership in Cleveland was expanding, there were 440 signed contracts "which the rank and file not only allowed but demanded." While theoretically opposed to contracts, the Hungarian-language branch did not reject them; to oppose them meant losing job control and opposing success.[25]

There are many points of view on the issue of the IWW and its disdain for some of the practical requirements of building a trade union in postwar America. Jean Tussey was an activist in the Socialist Workers Party of the United States (until her expulsion in 1984) and in her local union, Cleveland Typographical Union Local 53. Her husband, Richard Tussey (1918–1981), was the treasurer of Cleveland IWW Local 440 at a time when two issues came to a head. The first issue was the matter of signed "time agreements" and the second was whether or not to sign the non-Communist affidavits required by the Taft Hartley Act of 1947, which had only recently been passed. Worthman offers the following:

Disagreement between Cleveland 440 and the national IWW over accepting the Taft-Hartley law was the chief and last difficulty. Passed in 1947 by a Republican Congress over Truman's veto, the Taft-Hartley law banned closed shops, prohibited unions from calling strikes over jurisdictional strikes with other unions, allowed the President to declare injunctions in strikes which harmed the national interest, and required labor union officials to sign non-Communist affidavits. The old disagreement about contracts flared into a fundamental disagreement over Taft-Hartley in 1949 and 1950. Cleveland 440, rather than capitulate, chose to end its affiliation with the national IWW.[26]

Jean Tussey stressed the importance of accepting the existing trade union movement and working within it, despite its many faults. Cleveland 440 became affiliated with the Mechanics Educational Society of America (MESA), the president of which was Matthew Smith, who had a background in the British syndicalism of Tom Mann. MESA merged with the Meatcutters Union, which later merged with the Retail Clerks to form the United Food and Commercial Workers (UFCW).

Richard Tussey died of cancer in 1981. At the time of his death, he was an international representative of the UFCW.

Fred Thompson (1900–1987) was a member of the rejuvenated Socialist Party that was formed in 1973 in Milwaukee, after the three-way split in the old Socialist Party described earlier. Fred Thompson was also a longtime IWW organizer and author of the pamphlet *The Workers Who Built Cleveland;* he came to Cleveland in the late 1940s to help Cleveland IWW Local 440 cope with the challenges caused by demands for workplace contractualism on the one hand and anti-Communism on the other. Fred Thompson related that since the Cleveland IWW 440 had not signed the anti-Communist affidavits required by the Taft-Hartley Act, it could not participate in NLRB elections. He also mentioned the successful efforts of the USWA-CIO to displace the IWW at Jones and Laughlin Steel in Cleveland.[27]

The purpose of this brief detour into the history of the IWW in Ohio is simply to point out that a critique of the business unionism of the existing unions is not enough. One must also ask about the past experiences of those workers who were committed to a more militant and uncompromising form of trade unionism when confronted by the demand of some conservative workers for immediate results. To ignore these demands might invite a raid from more conservative trade unions promising to "deliver the goods." This was the experience of militant Wobblies in Ohio right after World War II. Some, when forced to choose between the uncompromising syndicalism of the national IWW and the need for compromises in order for a local to remain viable, chose the latter course. Thus the question needs to be asked of Staughton: "How would solidarity unionism respond to challenges such as those described above?"

We have examined Staughton's concept of solidarity unionism. Based on his own experiences with trade union leaders in the USWA and his own values, shaped through a variety of experiences going back to Macedonia as well as through conversations with men like John Sargent and Marty Glaberman, Staughton advocated and sought to bring into being organizations like the Workers Solidarity Club where workers would practice a nonauthoritarian and horizontal relationship both within the organization and with like-minded workers' organizations. While solidarity unionism received some sympathetic

criticism from activists like former organizer Colin Bossen, it continues to inspire the work of others in the same orbit of libertarian socialist and syndicalist communities. In a recent issue of *The Industrial
Worker* (the newspaper of the IWW), for example, one of Staughton's
collaborators, Daniel Gross, makes reference to Staughton's important
ideas on solidarity unionism. While studies like Roy Worthman's book
on the IWW in Ohio point out the complicated issues faced by those
within the IWW who were committed to anarcho-syndicalist values
and practices, one should not view solidarity unionism as impractical
and impossible to implement.

Chapter Nine ~⌒

STRUGGLE AND SOLIDARITY

"From 'Steel City' to 'A Nice Place to do Time.' . . ."

SHERRY LINKON AND JOHN RUSSO

Admirable Radical

In 1996, Staughton and Alice Lynd retired from Northeast Ohio Legal Services. Staughton had worked there since being fired in 1978 by a law firm that represented many labor unions in the Youngstown area. Alice joined Staughton at NOLS in 1985, after graduating from law school, and they both worked as attorneys there until retirement. The Lynds have many happy memories of their work at NOLS. As they entered retirement, they lived alone since their youngest child, Martha, who had been nine when the Lynds moved from Chicago, was now almost thirty and had moved away. The Lynds now began a period of prolific writing and traveling as well as activism.

It will come as no surprise that Alice and Staughton opposed both invasions of Iraq by the United States and its coalition forces. The first invasion came in 1991, during the presidency of George H. W. Bush, and the second came in the spring of 2003, during the presidency of his son, George W. Bush. In 2003, Staughton and Alice attended a meeting of Historians Against the War (HAW). At the meeting, Staughton met Carl Mirra, a young veteran and academic who later compiled an oral history of the first Iraq war.[1] The result was a friendship and collaboration that resulted in Mirra writing the first biography of Staughton Lynd, *The Admirable Radical*, published by Kent State University Press in 2010. Mirra's study, although focused on Staughton, covered such pivotal events as the time both of them spent in the Macedonia Cooperative Community and the civil rights movement, as well as Staughton's 1965 trip to Hanoi with Tom Hayden and Herbert Aptheker, and his role as a radical historian within the American Historical Association (AHA). It was natural for both Alice and Staughton to want someone to undertake a study of their life in Ohio, from the point where Mirra's study ended. It was their hope that such a study would focus on both Staughton and Alice in the years since 1976. After the first person wanting to write this second study disappeared, the Lynds entered into discussions with Kent State University librarians Mark Weber and Steve Paschen. In the fall of 2009, we began the project, conducting the first interview with Alice and Staughton that November. However, Alice and Staughton did not wait for others to tell their story. In 2009, they cowrote *Stepping Stones: Memoir of a Life Together*, chronicling their memories of living together over sixty years. A year later, Staughton wrote *Accompanying: Pathways to Social Change*, a reflection on accompaniment as an alternative to what he calls "the organizing model" used by activists both on the left and in the labor movement.

Kent State University

In one of Staughton's first cases as a lawyer, he represented faculty members at Kent State University who were opposing construction of a new gymnasium that would cover part of the ground where protesting students were killed by the National Guard on 4 May 1970. As mentioned previously, Staughton gave an address, "Oral History, Labor History and May 4," to the Friends of the Kent State University Library on 15 April 1998, an occasion that began a long relationship between the Lynds and the University Library. Jeanne Somers, then the curator of special collections, wrote to Staughton, thanking him for his remarks:

> A colleague of mine met with Kent State University President Cartwright early this morning and reported to me that, utterly outside of the context of their meeting, the President commented on your presentation and confided that you had changed her way of thinking about May 4th. I do not mean to imply that President Cartwright has ever been resistant to exploring the implications of May 4th. In fact, my own view is that her attitude toward the shootings is essentially reverential. I simply want to point out that, through your remarks, she came to some new awareness. I think that many of us experienced

a similar sense of being led, through your comments on the construct-
ing of history-from-the inside, to our own personal reconstructions
of those events, and, more importantly, to thoughts of our own individual roles in the legacy of May 4th as it is being lived today.

Jeanne Somers then worked with the Lynds to arrange for some of the
couple's papers to be deposited in the Department of Special Collections
and Archives. In 2000, Staughton joined anti-Vietnam War activist Jerry
Gordon, pacifist Larry Gara, and former Kent State SDS activist Candy
Erickson on a panel to discuss the 4 May shootings on the thirtieth anniversary of the tragedy. The panel discussion featured some moving
comments from the audience by a friend of the Lynds, Carl Oglesby
(1935–2011), an SDS activist and author of *Containment and Change.*
The Lynds were invited to the Kent State campus on other occasions, notably to meet old comrades, including SNCC activist Bob Moses, who spoke on campus in 2005, and former SDS leader Todd Gitlin,
who spoke there in 2010. Both programs were organized by library dean
Mark Weber. Alice and Staughton also spoke at the library's commemo-
ration of Black History Month in 2001. Staughton spoke on the civil
rights movement, and then he and Alice led the audience in singing
some spirituals associated with it.
In 2002, the Lynds helped to organize a conference at Kent State
University on the prospects for generating a "third New Left." On 27
August 2001, both Lynds met with other activists in the Kent State
University Library to plan a conference for the following June. Along
with the Lynds, the group included Al Haber, the first president of
the Students for a Democratic Society; historian Peter Linbaugh of
the University of Toledo; Micaela Brennan, Peter's wife; Eric O'Neil,
a construction worker from the Cincinnati area; Eric Kerl, a printer
from Cincinnati; and Mark Weber. Following this planning meeting,
Alice and Staughton worked with Mark Weber on the details of the
conference, scheduled for 30 May to 2 June of the following year. The
conference featured no big name speakers, instead bringing together a
remarkable collection of activists focused on sharing their experiences.
In addition to such planners of the event as the Lynds, Al Haber, Eric
O'Neil, and Peter Linbaugh, the seventy-five or so attendees included
Mike Stout (labor activist and former steelworker), Alexis Buss (then a
leader of the IWW), and others. While the conference did not stimulate

any overt rise in grassroots activity on college campuses or workplaces, the activists who came brought to the gathering their own experiences and insights, which proved to be much more meaningful than the sleep-inducing speeches by trade union or movement "leaders" that often were a feature of earlier left-wing and union conferences.

Youngstown Conferences, 1997–1999

Before the 2002 conference at Kent State, Alice and Staughton were among the initiators of three other conferences that took place in the Youngstown-Warren area between 1997 and 1999. The last of these was a conference entitled "Solidarity Unionism and Independent Working-class Politics," held in Youngstown between 4 and 6 June 1999. It featured a range of sessions, including "Beating Back the Global Economic Crisis," "Struggles in Local Unions," "The Development of Workers Centers and Community-Wide Struggles," and "Independent Working-class Electoral Campaigns." Staughton and longtime comrade Charlie McCollester chaired some of the sessions. The singing was provided by another veteran collaborator, Mike Stout, and his Human Union Band. About fifty trade unionists and other activists attended, participating in the sessions and discussing a number of resolutions.

At the 2002 Kent State University conference, it was clear to Mark Weber that neither Alice nor Staughton "controlled" or "dominated" the conference. Instead, Staughton especially spoke with a directness and sincerity that both projected a kind of moral authority and commanded the attention of even the most skeptical attendees. The same was probably true of the Youngstown area conferences.

Nicaragua, 1985–1990

Foreign travel has been an important part of the lives of both Alice and Staughton Lynd. The most dramatic journey in which Staughton engaged was probably his 1965 trip, with SDS leader Tom Hayden and Marxist historian Herbert Aptheker, to North Vietnam.[2] This trip brought down condemnations on the three participants from a number of sources in the United States. In Staughton's case, Kingman Brewster, president of Yale University, released a statement to the press attacking him for criticizing U.S. policy in Vietnam while he was a guest of the

North Vietnamese. This trip probably was a factor in his blacklisting from jobs in several colleges and universities over the next ten years.

Less controversial but equally meaningful were the trips the Lynds made to Central America and to Israel/Palestine after their move to Youngstown. Between 1985 and 1990, the Lynds made five trips to the war-ravaged Central American nation of Nicaragua during the vacation time they received from their jobs. In 1979, the popular Sandinista National Liberation Front (Frente Sandinista de Liberación Nacional, a guerilla movement known by its acronym, FSLN) forced Nicaraguan dictator Anastasio Somosa Debayle (1925–1980) from power; he was later assassinated in Paraguay. Somosa's father, Anastasio Somoza Garcia (1896–1956), who began the Samoza family's forty-year hold on power in Nicaragua in 1936, had been responsible for the murder of nationalist guerilla fighter August Cesar Sandino (1895–1934) and the massacre of many of Sandino's men following a peace accord. FSLN fighters took the name "Sandinista" in memory of the slain guerilla leader. One of the Lynds' closest friends is Father Joe Mulligan, who lives in Nicaragua's capital, Managua. Father Mulligan took Alice and Staughton to El Bonete, a grouping of six cooperative villages where the Lynds stayed for a week on their first visit. This experience likely brought back memories of Macedonia.

The United States government provided funding for a group of anti-Sandinista fighters (called the Contras), based across the border in Honduras. When the U.S. Congress voted to cut off aid to the Contras, the Reagan administration sought to continue funding them secretly. Into this cauldron of revolution, civil war, and national reconstruction was born an American peace organization, Witness for Peace, whose members tried to place themselves between the *Contra* rebels and villages in order to prevent violence and bloodshed. Witness for Peace would grow, after the wars in Nicaragua and El Salvador, to organize the lead delegations to many countries in Central and South America. The Lynds' youngest child, Martha Lynd Altan, visited Guatemala, her future home, as part of a Witness for Peace delegation. Gail Phares, one of the group's founders, remembered both the organization's beginnings and Father Mulligan, who took part in several of the yearly demonstrations and vigils at the School of the Americas near Fort Benning, Georgia.[3] At a party marking the Lynds' sixtieth wedding anniversary, Father Joe Mulligan helped celebrate the occasion.

Manuela Tambriz, center, posed for this photo with Alice and Staughton Lynd, taken during one of the Lynds' trips to Nicaragua. Kent State University Libraries. Special Collections and Archives.

The Lynds last visited Nicaragua in 1990, when they noted the exhaustion of many campesinos and workers after decades of war.[4] This was the year that the center-right forces led by Violetta Chomorro defeated the Sandinistas in national elections and took power. U.S. financial support, through organizations such as the National Endowment for Democracy (NED) was a significant factor in the Chomorro victory over Daniel Ortega and the Sandinistas.

While the Lynds have not returned to Nicaragua, their interest in Latin America continues. They had long admired the work of Archbishop Romero in El Salvador before his assassination in 1980 and were much taken by the January 1994 revolt of the Zapatista forces in the southernmost of Mexico's states, Chiapas. They applauded the announcement by the Zapatista leadership that they would not march on Mexico City and did not have the goal of trying to wield power over others. Finally, they traveled to Guatemala to visit their daughter Martha and to learn of Martha's work with women weavers.

Israel/Palestine

A second travel destination for Alice and Staughton Lynd was the occupied West Bank of the Jordan River, called Palestine by Arab residents there and Judea and Samaria by the Israeli settler community, which has greatly expanded its presence in this disputed land. The Israeli occupation of the West Bank began in 1967, making it one of the longest foreign occupations in recent history.

In Youngstown, Alice and Staughton, partly through their opposition to the first Gulf War, met and worked with many people from the Arab American community. One of these community leaders was a Palestinian Arab named Sami Bahour. "During Gulf War I," Staughton recalled, "we helped to organize a series of weekly meetings on conscientious objection and topics related to military counseling. We planned to repeat the series, and had reserved the space in the basement of the Cathedral in Youngstown, when the Gulf War ended. Someone suggested that we continue the weekly meetings but change the topics to the Holocaust, Palestine, Lebanon, Middle Eastern poetry, and other topics about which a few of us had a lot of personal knowledge and most of us knew nothing."[5]

Staughton went on to describe an event that both he and Alice found especially moving and meaningful:

> That year, Easter, Passover, and Ramadan fell at almost the same time. The idea presented itself of an occasion at the Arab-American Community Center in Youngstown devoted to the sharing of experiences. There would be no political speeches, attendees were instructed. It was a magical evening. Our friend and future colleague in prison lawsuits, Jules Lobel, described a visit to Israel. During the day, he collected accounts of civil rights violations in the West Bank. In the evenings, he spent time with members of his father's family, who had lived in the area since the eighteenth century. Their political positions ranged from ardent support for a greater Israel from the Mediterranean Sea to the Jordan River, to opposition to service in an occupying army in the West Bank.[6]

Sami Bahour spoke movingly at this event, and his friendship with the Lynds set the stage for their first trip to Israel/Palestine in the summer of 1991 in the company of Bahour's son, Sam.

Alice and Staughton returned to the area during the following summer. Their conversations with Palestinian Arabs in the West Bank, as well as earlier conversations with members of the Youngstown area Arab American community, resulted in a series of oral histories, published as *Homeland.*[7] The Lynds traveled to the West Bank, Gaza, and the Golan Heights, sometimes in areas not often visited by Westerners. They talked with ordinary Palestinian farmers and workers as well as activists. These people spoke of the difficulties, extreme in some cases, of life under the occupation of the Israeli Defense Forces (IDF). These difficulties included the bulldozing of homes and human rights abuses, which have been documented by international agencies such as Human Rights Watch.[8]

Upon their return to the United States, Alice and Staughton maintained their newly built friendship and collaboration with Youngstown-area Arab Americans. On 3 October 1997, the Lynds were honored at a dinner given by the Youngstown Islamic Center.[9] Writing in *Stepping Stones*, Alice and Staughton summarized their views on Israel and Palestine. They stated that continued Israeli occupation of the West Bank, with ongoing expansion of settlements, is likely to make a two-state solution almost impossible.[10] However, in the final section of their conclusions, Alice and Staughton seem to move beyond the two-state solution toward a one-state solution. Staughton writes as follows: "Remote as its realization may seem at present, the single, secular and bi-national state advocated by Jews such as Martin Buber and by the Palestine Liberation Organization when it was founded, seems in the long run the inevitable solution for all concerned. Any demographic disadvantage that might be experienced by Israelis in such a single nation would be slight when compared to the minority status of previously dominant whites in the new South Africa."[11]

Increasingly, there are dissenting voices both in Israel and the West. In two of his books, *The Invention of the Jewish People* and *The Invention of the Land of Israel*, Israeli scholar Shlomo Sand argues that there is no such thing as a seamless "Israeli citizenship"; there is citizenship for Jews and there is a kind of citizenship for Israeli Arabs. However, there is no secular state that provides equal protection under law to all citizens regardless of ethnicity or religion. The thinking of several post-Zionist scholars, such as Sand, would seem to point not toward a secular, bi-national state but rather toward a secular state with no nationalities committed to granting equal protection and equal rights to all citizens, regardless of ethnicity or religion. No doubt the Lynds would support such a goal.[12]

The debate over which is more just, Jewish state or a secular bi-national state, should not obscure the fact that the friendship betweem the Lynds and the Bahour family, both in Youngstown and on the West Bank, provided Alice and Straughton with the opportunity to edit, with Sam Bahour, a volume of interviews with Palestinian Arabs, chronicling their lives and struggles on the West Bank, that was published as *Homeland.* Alice and Staughton traveled to the West Bank twice to visit the Bahour family and to listen to the experiences of other Arab families.[13] This was done both in the spirit of history from below and in the spirit of accompaniment. What *Rank and File* did for our consciousness of the memories and experiences of American rank-and-file workers, *Homeland* did for the average Palestinian Arab families living under the occupation. The Lynds' friendship with the Bahour family and others in the West Bank/Palestine continues since *Homeland*'s publication in 1994.

In an interview on 11 September 2013, Jules Lobel stated that the issue of the rights of Palestinian Arabs on the West Bank of the Jordan River became yet another opportunity for him to collaborate with the Lynds. A tear gas company located near Pittsburgh was selling their product to the Israeli Defense Force, which in turn sprayed some of the tear gas into the homes of Palestinian Arab families living on the West Bank. The resultant injuries to many provoked protests by Palestinian Arabs living in Youngstown. Between 1988 and 1990, they filed suit in court to stop the Pittsburgh company from selling its tear gas to Israel. The plaintiffs won initially but lost on appeal when the court ruled that since the Palestinian plaintiffs were not citizens of the United States, they had no legal standing in U.S. courts.[14]

New Local Challenges and Directions

In the Youngstown of the late 1980s and early 1990s, all the steel mills were silent. The steel companies had left town, leaving in their wake unemployed workers and their families and steeply rising rates of poverty and crime. Ten years after the shutdowns, the community had not begun to recover. Moreover, as Sherry Lee Linkon and John Russo observed,

> the landscape was also changed by the social and psychological costs of the shutdowns. Youngstown's primary community mental health center, Parkview Counseling Center, saw a threefold increase in its caseload in the 1980s with significant increases in depression, child and spouse abuse, drug and alcohol abuse, divorces, and suicides. Even the caseworkers struggled with the emotional aftershocks of the shutdowns. Unable to deal with the increased caseloads, many became frustrated and isolated from friends and peers, and nobody took care of the caretakers.[15]

As crime and related psychological maladies continued to increase in Youngstown, some saw the growth of a prison economy in the Youngstown area as a solution. Between 1992 and 1998, four new prisons were built in the Mahoning Valley. These prison facilities, according to Linkon and Russo, "boosted payrolls, tax revenue, and overall economic activity."[16] While some Mahoning Valley communities and neighborhoods welcomed the prisons as a source of jobs, others opposed the establishment of lockdown facilities in the midst of residential neighborhoods where children played and where many senior citizens lived alone in homes or apartments. One prison that drew considerable comment and criticism was the Northeast Ohio Correctional Center (NEOCC), located on the north end of Youngstown. The NEOCC was established as a private prison facility by the Correctional Corporation of America (CCA). "One of the new prisons," noted Linkon and Russo, "the privately owned Northeast Ohio Corrections Center on Youngstown's north side, had a series of problems, including assaults, a murder, and the midday escape of six prisoners."[17] Several years later, in 2001, the CCA closed its facility in Youngstown, but by that time the issue of prisons and the rights of prisoners had become a new focus for Alice and Staughton.

Between 1985 and 2002, Alice and Staughton worked together not only as the comrades they had always been but also as attorneys and activists. They visited several countries, including Nicaragua and Israel/Palestine, and even after retiring as attorneys in 1996, they remained active on many fronts. They organized conferences on issues such as

solidarity unionism and prospects for the rebirth of a New Left. As an
outreach of the Workers Solidarity Club, Staughton and other collaborators edited a monthly newsletter, *Impact,* that reached out initially to
rank-and-file labor activists and their academic supports and then those
incarcerated in prison.

Chapter Ten ⌒◯

LUCASVILLE

"When it comes to working with inmates, Alice is a saint."

JULES LOBEL

Prisoners

During the period 1999–2001, Mark Weber subscribed to the newsletter *Impact*. For its first eighty-five issues (over about eight years),
Impact was sponsored by the Youngstown Workers Solidarity Club. In
its April 2000 issue, however, an editorial statement appearing under
the title, "Staughton Lynd, A Personal Letter," signaled a change. Ob-
serving that prisoners accounted for more than half of *Impact*'s readers, Staughton stated that "in seeking a readership that includes both
rank-and-file workers and prisoners, we assist one group of oppressed
persons, who are primarily white, to understand a little better the experience of another group of oppressed persons, in very large numbers
black."[1] While the newsletter had published the letters of prisoners for
several years, this was an explicit statement that the newsletter saw
a connection between the lives of workers and the lives of prisoners.
As Staughton noted, however, some readers wanted the publication to
remain a labor newsletter: "The purpose of the newsletter remains . . .
to build solidarity among rank-and-file workers in the Mahoning Valley and throughout the country. But the purpose has changed over the
years. The auto workers who helped to create *Impact*, one of whom
gave the newsletter its name, felt that the newsletter should stick to
trade union issues. 'Don't write articles about Palestine,' one of them
said. Other members of the editorial group, however, considered internationalism to be a necessary aim of any publication for workers."

Staughton speaks at an informal forum in 2006. Kent State University Libraries. Special Collections and Archives.

Staughton's personal letter went on to summarize the state of things during the twenty-odd years since the steel mill shutdowns. Three organizations examined earlier in this book (Workers Solidarity Club, Solidarity USA, and Workers Against Toxic Chemicals) no longer existed by the year 2000. In part, this happened because key activists had died, moved away, were experiencing health problems, or were caught up in other activities and responsibilities. Staughton concluded by reminding readers that participatory democracy, or self-activity, is not just for workers; prisoners need it as well.[2] This letter, with Staughton's customary openness, seemed to illustrate that the issue of prisoners' rights and prisons was becoming a larger issue in the lives of the Lynds.

The ACLU

The National Civil Liberties Bureau (NCLB) was founded in 1917 in the midst of a government crackdown on those individuals and groups that opposed U.S. participation in World War I. In 1920, the organization was succeeded by the American Civil Liberties Union (ACLU). Founded by Roger Baldwin, Crystal Eastman, and Walter Nelles, the ACLU focused defending the rights of antiwar protesters and those who were being persecuted by the government because of their political beliefs. This was the era of the postwar Red Scare, which saw the jailing of socialist orator Eugene V. Debs because of an antiwar speech he delivered in Canton, Ohio in 1918 and the deportation of such radicals as Emma Goldman and Alexander Berkman. Since that time, the ACLU has worked to defend the rights of striking workers, draft resisters, and political dissidents, artists, students, and prisoners, gay people and racial minorities. It has supported the separation of church and state, fought creationism in the courts, and opposed those provisions of antiterrorism legislation that undermine the civil liberties of citizens. It has also supported abortion rights and access to birth control.

The Lynds have had various connections with the ACLU over their adult lives. On several occasions, Staughton has been an ACLU client, while both Alice and Staughton have served many times as volunteer attorneys for the ACLU of Ohio.

During a demonstration on the steps of the Pentagon on 9 August 1965 (the twentieth anniversary of Nagasaki Day), Staughton was arrested and received representation from the ACLU. In December 1965, Staughton, along with Tom Hayden of the SDS and Marxist historian Herbert Aptheker, defied a State Department travel ban by traveling to North Vietnam. Mel Wulf of the ACLU, along with Alice, met Staughton at the airport on his return from North Vietnam, just in case federal officials were planning to arrest him.[3]

Several months later, David Carliner, another ACLU attorney and an expert in immigration law, worked with Staughton to retrieve his passport after it was seized by the U.S. government. The government wanted to establish that Staughton had used his passport to get into North Vietnam; when this effort failed, Staughton's passport was returned to him.

At the 1968 Democratic Party Convention in Chicago, the city's mayor, Richard Daley, issued directives severely restricting First Amendment rights. Staughton led a march in protest and ended up getting arrested. The ACLU provided his defense. While Staughton wanted his case to be argued on First Amendment grounds, in the end he simply pleaded guilty and paid a fine.

As attorneys, Alice and Staughton worked for the ACLU on two separate occasions. The most extensive legal work they undertook for the organization concerned a class action brought to challenge conditions of confinement at the Ohio State Penitentiary (OSP) and procedures for placement and retention of Ohio prisoners at the highest level of security (discussed below). In addition, the Lynds filed four "friend of the court" briefs as volunteer attorneys for the ACLU of Ohio on behalf of members of the Lucasville Five, leaders in a prison riot at the maximum security prison in Lucasville who had been sentenced to death.[4]

Most recently, in 2011, Staughton served as an attorney for Occupy Youngstown when some Youngstown citizens challenged a local ordinance that prohibited the blocking of sidewalks but which was interpreted in such a manner as to compromise the rights of those peaceful demonstrators who were part of the local Occupy movement.

The Lucasville Prison Uprising

In the course of their work with prisoners, both Alice and Staughton faced challenges that would test their courage and their commitment. Their work on behalf of the inmates referred to as the Lucasville Five added a new dimension to the accompaniment work they had done on behalf of steelworkers, retirees, the poor, and Palestinian Arabs struggling against Israel's occupation of the West Bank. In every case except perhaps that of the Palestinian Arabs, their legal training allowed Alice and Staughton to provide concrete service to those in need.

In the first few months of 1993, most Americans were preoccupied with the beginning of the presidency of former Arkansas governor Bill Clinton, whose election to the White House had ended twelve years of GOP control of the executive branch of government. Then in April of that year, national television coverage was focused on the horror of the U.S. government's raid on the Branch Davidian compound near Waco, Texas. Accordingly, outside of Ohio, most people took only scant notice of the longest prison uprising in America history, which took place within the Southern Ohio Correctional Facility (SOCF) in Lucasville, a small Ohio town of about 1500 people.

On the eve of the prison uprising, which began on 11 April 1993, the SOCF employed about 650 corrections staff and related employees, many of whom were represented by the Ohio Civil Service Employees Association (OCSEA), Local 11 of the American Federation of State, County, and Municipal Employees.[5] There was, perhaps, more than a little irony in the fact that the Lucasville uprising pitted unionized workers (correctional officials) against a mostly minority inmate population.

The inmates at the Lucasville prison rose in outrage about overcrowding and intolerable living conditions. During the uprising, one officer, Robert Vallandingham, and nine inmates were killed. One of the inmates killed was a man named Earl Elder. Eventually, through negotiations and the pacifying efforts of a number of inmates, the rebellion ended. In its wake, authorities determined to hold someone responsible identified five inmates of the SOCF as ringleaders. All five, soon known in the press as the Lucasville Five, were eventually convicted of aggravated murder and sentenced to death.

Supermax

In 1996, following their official retirement as attorneys for NOLS, Alice and Staughton became involved in an effort to learn more about a supermax prison scheduled to be built in or near Youngstown. "We knew nothing about 'supermax prisons' or 'control units' where prisoners are kept in solitary confinement for twenty-three or twenty-four hours a day for years, and where physical and mental abuse is sometimes rampant," Alice later wrote. "I began reading all the articles I could obtain on conditions in supermaximum security prisons and the psychological effects of prolonged solitary confinement, not only on the prisoners but also on the guards in such prisons."[6]

Alice and Staughton initially worked with concerned students from Oberlin College on the issue of supermax prisons. At a public forum on such facilities, Alice read a paper on the effects of supermax prisons on both inmates and corrections officers. Together with some of the Oberlin students, Alice and Staughton later toured the nearly completed supermax prison near Youngstown.

At the same public forum on the supermax, Jackie Bowers was one of the speakers. Bowers is the sister of George Skatzes, one of the five inmates at the SOCF in Lucasville convicted as ringleaders of the 1993 prison uprising. She put the Lynds in touch with George Skatzes's attorney, and eventually they met Skatzes. Through him, the Lynds also met the other four members of the Lucasville Five, all sentenced to death for their alleged roles as leaders in the Lucasville uprising: Keith Lamar, Siddique Abdullah Hasan (formerly Carlos Sanders), Namir (formerly James Were), and Jason Robb. This began one of the most rewarding and challenging accompaniments of the Lynds' Ohio years as Alice and Staughton visited, listened to, counseled, and learned from three of the five, Skatzes, Robb, and Lamar.

George, Jason, and Keith

Over the years, these three men changed and Alice and Staughton changed with them. The Lynds worked to get them competent legal counsel, filed briefs on their behalf (one of which concerned the expanded right of discovery), and became their friends when they had few others. Lawyers for the men have come and gone, but Alice and Staughton have remained—one of the few constants in their lives. Even now, twenty years after the Lucasville revolt, Alice and Staughton maintain their contacts with all five. This is not "legal representation" but accompaniment: the Lynds are identifying with the lives of those who are poor and oppressed. On 9 September 2013, at their home in Niles, both Lynds spoke with the authors of their ongoing relationship with George, Jason, and Keith. Midway through the conversation, the telephone rang. Since Staughton was talking at the moment, Alice rose to answer the phone. She returned from the call fifteen minutes later to say the caller was Jason Robb.

In the fall of 2012, the authors visited both Keith LaMar and Jason Robb at the Ohio State Penitentiary in Youngstown. Both men are in their mid-forties and have been in prison since they were teenagers. Both are under sentence of death for their alleged roles in the 1993 Lucasville uprising. Keith LaMar fondly remembered his first meeting with Alice and Staughton Lynd around 1996, before he was transferred to the prison in Youngstown. He recalled that they actually listened to him and took his ideas about his case seriously.[7] Jason Robb also praised the Lynds, not only for their work on behalf of his case but also because of their efforts to make his life "on the inside" more bearable.[8]

Alice remembered the alarming restrictions that were placed on George Skatzes during visitation: "On our next visit, George was wearing a 'black box' that held his hands and arms in a rigid position, with one hand above the other, the upper hand facing up and the lower hand facing down, so that it was impossible to use the hands in coordination with each other. It was years before we were able to get the administration to stop using the black box routinely during visits."[9]

Gradually, over the years, Alice and Staughton built up a bond of trust between themselves and the inmates at the OSP in Youngstown. In October 2012, when the authors interviewed Keith LaMar for the second time, LaMar commented that "Alice and Staughton, they are like family, man."[10] Such a relationship embodies the the radical organizer's accompaniment goal of becoming friends with the oppressed rather than seeing them simply as actors in some larger historical drama.

Austin v. Wilkinson

The suicide of death row inmates at the OSP in Youngstown in the first few months of 1998 deeply troubled the Lynds and led them to contact Professor Jules Lobel of the Law School at the University of Pittsburgh. Lobel had been one of Alice's teachers in law school and he was affiliated with the Center for Constitutional Rights in New York City.[11] With the CCR obtaining grant funding to cover some of the costs of litigation, Alice and Staughton approached the Ohio ACLU in Cleveland about getting local counsel to address the due process issues of the case, including the methods and procedures used by the State of Ohio to determine which inmates should be housed in the OSP in Youngstown.

Perhaps some background on the Center for Constitutional Rights would be useful. Originally founded in 1966 as the Law Center for Constitutional Rights, it took its current name when it merged with the Emergency Civil Liberties Committee (ECLC). Jules Lobel, the CCR's current president, spoke about the focus of the organization in a September 2013 interview. He stated that the CCR was formed initially to fight for the rights of civil rights workers in the South who were being harassed and beaten by local law enforcement. The CCR, he stated, sees itself as the legal voice of the civil rights movement and its goal is to use the courts to advance that movement's goals. The CCR will take a case not necessarily because it can be won in court but because the very act of going to court will bring media attention to the issue being litigated. Lobel contrasted the CCR with the ACLU, which seeks to bring winnable cases to court in order to extend legal precedents and further develop the law on a particular issue.[12]

One of the founders of the CCR, Arthur Kinoy, was also a leader of another organization, the National Lawyers Guild (NLG). In the spring of 2013, the authors accompanied Alice and Staughton to a guild conference held at the Case Western Reserve Law School, where both Lynds spoke about issues related to prisoners' rights. The focus of the NLG differs from that of the ACLU and the CCR. While the last two groups both seek to litigate, the NLG is primarily an educational organization which sponsors conferences and programs and has chapters at some law schools around the country. The conservative counterpart to the NLG is the Federalist Society, which likewise has chapters at some law schools.

To return to the case, in January 2011, after more than two years of preparation, Alice and Staughton Lynd and the other lawyers representing the prisoners filed a lawsuit in United States District Court, *Austin v. Wilkinson*. The suit charged that conditions in the OSP-Youngstown were an "atypical and significant hardship" that the inmates should not have to endure. In particular, the suit addressed the hardships imposed on prisoners by solitary confinement; such prisoners were denied not only social contact with other inmates but also due process rights, in terms of the procedures used to determine which inmates should go to solitary confinement. As Jules Lobel recalls, he drafted the brief while Alice and Staughton worked with the testimony of the prisoners and developed the factual record during the trial. Both Lynds were very good at working with the prisoners, in part because they were already very familiar with conditions inside the Supermax One of their most important contributions to this case was the extraordinary lengths to which they went in order to contact inmates and obtain documents from them about conditions at the OSP. The Lynds and Lobel received assistance from two Cleveland attorneys, Terry Gilbert and Mike Benza.

Austin v. Wilkinson became one of the leading cases in helping to establish and define the due process rights of inmates in solitary confinement. The plaintiffs won at the U.S. District Court and on appeal. As a result of the litigation, Ohio state prisons undertook the construction of outdoor recreation facilities and improved access to medical care. On the issue of the rights of inmates to due process in determining whether or not they should be in solitary confinement, the State of Ohio appealed to the U.S. Supreme Court. By a 9–0 vote, the court upheld the right of an inmate to a due process hearing before being sent into solitary confinement. However, the court said the hearing could be "minimal."

Alice and Staughton Work with Inmates

Both Keith LaMar and Jason Robb emphasized in interviews how much it meant to them that Alice and Staughton consistently consulted with the inmates and sought evidence from them. Alice estimates that from 2001, when *Austin v. Wilkinson* was filed, through 2008, she and Staughton corresponded with more than six hundred of the one thousand-odd inmates at the OSP-Youngstown.[13] The suit was placed on an expedited track despite efforts by the lawyers for the State of Ohio to delay the process. In the meantime, the State of Ohio began to make some efforts to monitor the health of inmates and to improve recreational facilities in prisons.

In an interview with Keith LaMar, we learned of the depth of the inmates' appreciation and respect for the Lynds' work to improve prison conditions.[14] At a celebration of the Lynds' sixtieth wedding anniversary at Youngstown's Catholic Worker house, a letter from Keith LaMar was read out loud. In the letter, he called Alice "Mama Bear" and Staughton, "Scrapper," affectionate nicknames given the Lynds by the inmates for their dogged pursuit of better prison living conditions for the prisoners. Eventually, the U.S. Court of Appeals and the U.S. Supreme Court ruled in favor of the inmates' suit, concluding that the OSP environment was an atypical and significant hardship and that the inmates had a "liberty interest" in trying to avoid being sent to the prison to serve their sentences.

In their work with prisoners in Ohio, Alice and Staughton Lynd exhibited the following principles of accompaniment: radical equality, listening, seeking consensus, and acts of moral witness to injustice.[15]

"Listen to me! Shut your mouth! Leave everything to me and stop with all the questions. I'll get back to you when I know something." This is the stereotypical advice given to an inmate by his attorney in countless films and novels. Today, perhaps, the message is more muted, but the theme is the same: we are your lawyers and we know the system. Leave your fate in our hands and we will get back to you when we have something to report. The accompaniment approach of Alice and Staughton Lynd is different. Why? Because the Lynds, as organizers as well as lawyers, seek to establish with their "clients" a new relationship of radical equality. As Alice Lynd expressed it years earlier in her draft counseling work, there are two experts in the room and the lawyer is only one of the experts. The other expert is the inmate. The inmate is an expert on his or her life and experiences and the lawyer or organizer has as much to learn from the inmate as the inmate has to learn from the lawyer or organizer. Without this mutual openness to learn from one another, there cannot be the radical equality that is the basis of accompaniment work among prisoners.

If the radical equality just mentioned does not exist, then the listening done by the lawyer will not be foundational but rather only tactical. It becomes something that the lawyer must endure or get through in order to direct the inmate toward a predetermined set of strategies or goals. If the listening is foundational, however, then the listening done by the lawyer or organizer and the inmate is reciprocal and leads to something called consensus. What is consensus?

Seeking consensus is a process by which, in the words of Barry Morley, "we open ourselves to being guided by the Light to a place where we can sit in unity in the collective inward Presence."[16] This means that the lawyer is not in complete control of the outcome. Instead, both lawyer and inmate(s) are moved together to a collective decision about what to do. In our interviews with inmates Keith LaMar and Jason Robb, both men expressed an appreciation and understanding of *why* Alice and Staughton Lynd seemed so interested in what they thought about particular issues—some merely procedural, some substantive, and some both—facing them in their many legal battles.[17]

The last principle of accompaniment requires the person involved to undertake some kind of act of moral witness to injustice. What kinds of acts are open to inmates in a prison system? Keith LaMar and Jason Robb made reference to a 2011 hunger strike they undertook with Siddique Abdullah Hasan (Carlos Sanders) in Ohio. In *Accompanying*, Staughton describes the hunger strike as being both interracial and successful, unlike many prison hunger strikes. In the Ohio hunger strike, the three Lucasville Five hunger strikers asked for the same privileges granted to other death row inmates. These included being permitted to sit together with visitors who come to see them and be allowed to give such visitors a hug (even while shackled and chained to the floor).[18]

Alice and Staughton Lynd related to the inmates at the OSP as attorneys committed to justice and to the principles of accompaniment. However, in Staughton's case, there is another dimension to this relationship—that of being a professional historian committed to both a search for truth and an approach to history from the bottom up, in which the story is told from the viewpoint of the oppressed as well as those of the prison authorities and state political readers. Perhaps the duty of the radical organizer who accompanies the inmates, the workers, or the poor is not only to "walk with them," but also to tell their story in cases where the oppressed cannot tell it themselves. Some inmates, such as Mumia Abu-Jamal (and Keith LaMar), are excellent writers; some, however, are not, and they depend on other people to tell of their experiences. In their accompaniment work, the Lynds have tried to tell the stories of those with whom they have walked. In the case of Youngstown steelworkers, they did so in the book *The Fight Against the Shutdown*. To tell the stories of Palestinians on the West Bank, they collaborated with Sam Bahour to collect and publish oral histories in *Homeland*. Finally, the story of the inmates found expression in *Lucasville: The Untold Story of a Prison Uprising*. In each and every case, regardless of whose name is on the cover of the book, the endeavor to "tell the story" is a cooperative and collaborative effort by both Alice and Staughton, side by side.

Mr. X

In August 2000, Alice and Staughton, as attorneys for Skatzes, went to see an inmate whom Alice calls Mr. X in her account in the joint memoir *Stepping Stones*. They asked him about some of the deaths that occurred during the Lucasville prison riot of 1993. Here is Alice's description of their first meeting with Mr. X: "We asked him about the murder of Officer Vallandingham. Mr. X brought up the Elder murder. 'George should not be punished for being innocent,' he said. He told us that three people had killed Earl Elder. He named two. Then I asked him, 'Do you want to tell me who the other guy was?' 'It was me,' he blurted out. He turned to his left, bent over, and sobbed. In seven years, he had not told anyone. He wanted to be at peace with himself."[19]

Following the meeting with Mr. X, Alice prepared an affidavit stating that while Mr. X's statements about the murder of Earl Elder (a prisoner) could be true, further investigation was needed and should take place.

Three years later, in September 2003, George Skatzes had a new attorney; the next month, she filed Alice's affidavit. Alice and Staughton informed Mr. X about the decision of George's new attorney to file the affidavit. The following spring (March 2004), Alice received a subpoena to appear in court to testify on 2 April 2004. A second subpoena directed her to bring to court all documents she had relating to her dealings with Mr. X. Alice prepared a short statement as to why she would refuse to testify. Among her reasons was the fact that her testimony could be considered "snitch testimony," and Alice, on principle, opposed the use of such testimony. She also stated that, as a Quaker, she was opposed to the death penalty and that she would not be a party to efforts to put another man (Mr. X) on death row.[20]

In October 2004, Alice received a grand jury subpoena. A month later, after informing the presiding judge at the grand jury hearing that she would not testify, Alice was ordered to jail by the judge. Although Alice entered jail and served time, she was quickly released when the Court of Appeals north of Portsmouth, Ohio, where the grand jury met, granted a stay in her sentencing to jail. In December 2004, to prevent Alice being sent back to jail for refusing to testify, Mr. X gave Alice permission to give limited testimony. Mr. X was convicted in 2005 and received a sentence of fifteen years to life, with credit for time served since 1993. Sadly, the testimony of Mr. X regarding his role in the murder of inmate Earl Elder did not benefit George Skatzes. He remains under conviction for the murder of Elder even though Mr. X testified to the contrary.

Alice took great pains to explain to George Skatzes and the other inmates why she was cooperating with the authorities. The entire ordeal was very hard on both Alice and Staughton. Staughton had recently turned seventy-five years old and Alice was on a special diet that would have been disrupted by a prison stay of longer than a day or two. Both benefited from the strong presence of their daughter Martha, as well as from the support of many friends and supporters from the Youngstown-Warren area.

Beginning in 1976, Alice and Staughton have been involved in two great struggles: the fight to prevent the shutdown of the Youngstown area steel mills and their legal advocacy on behalf of the Lucasville Five. The first struggle involved Staughton primarily, since Alice was often at home with their youngest child, Martha. During the Lucasville struggle, however, Alice and Staughton worked together, side by side. Alice risked going to prison to protect the confidentiality of her client. Both Lynds forged strong bonds of friendship with three of the Lucasville Five (Jason Robb, Keith LeMar, and George Skatzes). This friendship continues; even though Alice and Staughton no longer formally represent them legally, they still visit each of the three men. Moreover, they both remain involved in the work with prisoners and both still advocate for the abolition of the death penalty in Ohio.

Chapter Eleven

OCCUPY AND ACCOMPANY

> "'Accompanying' and 'Occupying' are first cousins, or
> perhaps, to speak more precisely, blood brothers."
>
> STAUGHTON LYND

Occupy: Some Participants Speak

Over the Labor Day weekend of 2012, one of the authors traveled to the Twin Oaks Community near Charlottesville, Virginia. At this annual conference of enthusiasts for intentional living communities and cohousing ventures, he attended a workshop on the Occupy Wall Street movement that had begun on 17 September 2011 and spread to cities all over the country. This workshop drew more than fifty people, mostly young, who had taken part in Occupy movements in the cities of New York City, Burlington, Vermont, West Palm Beach, Florida, Oakland, California, Washington, D.C., Charlottesville, Virginia, and New Orleans, Louisiana, as well as in Franklin County, Massachusetts.

The discussion focused on the personal experiences of the program attendees.[1] A woman named Sarah said the Occupy movement was important because it forced participants to take on the role of caring for space, not just listening to speeches. A woman named Beatrice asserted that in her experience with both Occupy Oakland and Occupy Wall Street, the movement empowered people like herself who had been marginalized in society. A third participant, Jessie, felt she learned a great deal from trying to make group decisions with people from very diverse backgrounds. To the question, "Would you participate in another Occupy movement?" most participants answered "yes," with the following three caveats: First, the movement would have to have a clearer long-term strategy. Second, it would have to do a much better job of forging links with the community surrounding the Occupy site. Third, the movement would have to be nonexclusionary.

While this response was echoed by many of the Occupy movement participants at the meeting, it was clear that these young people were not primarily students. Many had been to college and even to graduate school. Now they were finding that there were no jobs for them even though some labored under significant debt from student loans. In an interview outside his home, Staughton provided a similar analysis: "What's interesting to me is in contrast to the 60's, I don't think it's exactly students. I think the core is ex-students who have done everything they were supposed to: high school, college, and graduate school, and now they're out of school with a bunch of debts and unemployed."[2]

During the long season of GOP presidential debates in the fall of 2011, GOP candidate Newt Gingrich stated that those taking part in the Occupy Wall Street protest should "get a job." To many Occupy activists, it seems that a job is just what they were looking for and had given up hope of finding. They had done what they were supposed to do and now they were being told that their skills and services were not needed. They became part of the 99 percent of the movement's slogan.[3]

Occupy Youngstown

On 15 October 2011 in Youngstown, about a month after the start of Occupy Wall Street, Staughton spoke to about four hundred people at the opening rally of Occupy Youngstown. In his remarks, Staughton touched on several themes of the Occupy movement that seemed to strike at the heart of the politics of accompaniment that both Lynds have practiced over the entire span of their careers. He began with the theme of solidarity. Solidarity was a bond over time with the steelworkers like Ed Mann, who fought to start a community-owned steel mill in the Mahoning Valley. It was a connection with the Zapatistas, who had revolted against oppression, corruption, and NAFTA in the jungles of Southern Mexico. And it was a feeling of kinship with the dedicated efforts of the Lucasville Five—and indeed many other inmates—to fight against inhuman prison conditions and against the death penalty.

Staughton also addressed the frequent criticism of the Occupy movement that it had no program or demands. This was a charge with which Staughton was familiar. One of the early and most often-heard complaints about the Students for a Democratic Society and other New Left groups was that they had no demands and no list of reforms. Conventional wisdom was that without them, such groups could not be taken seriously. In response, Lynd said, "When our critics use the word 'demands,' they mean: tell some legislator or administrator what you want him to do for you. Gather your own initiative, your self-activity, and your righteous outrage into a bundle, and give it to someone else to act in your place. Tell someone else what you want them to do for you."[4] Staughton then offered an alternative plan: "We need to remake the world ourselves, right now, from below and to the left."[5] As Alice would say it, "Do whatever you can do about what you see as problems. Ask, 'What is the next step?'"

After the initial rally, the Occupy Youngstown movement (OY) established an ongoing presence on Federal Plaza in downtown Youngstown. Initially, the demonstrators used a tent for shelter and a barrel of combustible materials for warmth. In November 2011, Youngstown police officials confiscated the tent, the barrel, and some personal items (mostly clothing) found in the tent. As a legal justification for this act, the City of Youngstown cited City Ordinance 521.04(c). This ordinance states: "No person shall place, deposit or maintain any merchandise, goods, material or equipment upon any sidewalk so as to obstruct pedestrian traffic thereon."[6] Occupy Youngstown and several individual OY participants then filed suit against the City of Youngstown, the police chief, and the mayor. When the attorney representing OY withdrew from the case, Staughton and Alice Lynd stepped in as volunteer attorneys for the ACLU of Ohio. Staughton obtained and submitted photographs taken both by the city and by OY participants which clearly demonstrated that at the time the tent was taken down and confiscated, pedestrian traffic on Federal Plaza was not being obstructed.

On 31 May 2012, the city responded by filing a motion for summary judgment (dismissal) of the suit filed by Occupy Youngstown against it. Occupy Youngstown responded with a memorandum to the court opposing the motion for summary judgment. The local magistrate ruled in favor of the City of Youngstown on 30 July, 2 August, and 21 August 2012. In his last ruling for the city of Youngstown and against OY, the magistrate stated that OY should have known that an assembly permit would be required for its gathering on Federal Plaza. The end came on 14 September 2012, when Judge Scott Krichbaum upheld the ruling of the magistrate one month earlier and granted the motion by attorneys for the City of Youngstown for summary judgment.

In cities across the country, local police cracked down on the Occupy movement, evicting protesters from prominent sites like Federal Plaza in downtown Youngstown. Protesters, pundits, and politicians (as well as ordinary citizens) asked, "Okay, what's next?" The authors posed this question to Alice and Staughton at a recent meeting at their home.[7] Alice responded that her theme for decades has been building community. Community requires facing conflicts and working through them in the interest of shared goals and principles. Alice and Staughton have joined with former OY participant Thomas Sabatini in offering an exciting class on world history to prisoners at Ohio's Trumbull County Correctional Institution. Also, as an outgrowth of Occupy Youngstown encouraged by the Youngstown Diocese, Alice has offered a series of classes on crime, justice and the death penalty attended by several former Occupiers. Alice also contributed to the scholarly discussion of the death penalty in Ohio with her article, "Fair and Can't Be Fixed: The Machinery of Death in Ohio," which appeared in the fall 2012 edition of the *University of Toledo Law Review.*

Alice and Staughton offered support to and analysis of the Occupy movement, both nationally and locally, in Youngstown. They were active in trying, unsuccessfully, to prevent the City of Youngstown from tearing down and confiscating the tent and other materials belonging to the OY movement. It is to their credit that they did not romanticize the movement as the opening salvos of revolution but instead admitted that it was primarily a gathering of middle class, college-educated young people who "did everything right" and yet could find no employment. From here we take a look at Alice and Staughton today and their contributions.

Chapter Twelve ⌒◯

THE LYNDS TODAY

An Assessment

> "Inasmuch as ye have done it unto one of the least
> of these my brethren, ye have done it unto me."
>
> MATHEW 25:40, KJV

The House on Timbers Court

When the authors ring the doorbell at 1694 Timbers Court in Niles, an elderly man greets us warmly at the door. This is Staughton Lynd, eighty-three years old. Waiting for us inside is Alice Lynd, also eighty-three, Staughton's wife and partner for almost sixty-three years. Ushered into the small house, we take familiar seats in the kitchen. Staughton prepares strong black coffee for us. Alice does not drink coffee. We come with a prepared set of questions and we tape-record the Lynds' answers. Alice listens very keenly and comments while she knits or darns socks. Staughton does most of the talking. His responses to questions include stories and observations based on his long experience. Occasionally, Alice gently chides him to get to the point. Staughton receives these prompts good-naturedly and then proceeds with his narrative. Throughout our many visits with Alice and Staughton, we have experienced only openness, patience, and a willingness to share. Never have we been met with the response, "We prefer not to answer that question."

Alice and Staughton continue to do many activities together. For example, they are members of a singing group that meets regularly and occasional concerts, especially during the December holiday period. They also enjoy reading out loud together; during one of our interviews, Staughton remarked that he and Alice were reading Taylor Branch's book on America during the years when Martin Luther King was the most prominent civil rights leader in the country. Currently the Lynds are reading aloud a biography of Celia Sánchez, a heroine of the Cuban Revolution.

They both still write and edit books and articles. As we write this, Staughton's latest book is the aforementioned *Accompanying*, published by PM Press, while Alice has recently published an article on the death penalty in the *University of Toledo Law Review*.

They also remain active as teachers in very nontraditional settings. In early 2013, Staughton conducted a series of classes on the ideas of Archbishop Oscar Romero at the Youngstown Catholic Worker house. In early 2014, Alice presented a series of classes on law and justice in a community setting in Youngstown. She also presented a seminar mentioned earlier, "Crime, Justice and the Death Penalty," in both 2012 and 2013. As noted in chapter 11, the Lynds have also been teaching, together with historian and teacher Thomas Sabatini, a class on world history to prisoners at the Trumbull County Correctional Institution.

Friends and Comrades Speak

The close relationships the Lynds have forged over the years with their comrades in struggle continue even after a struggle is over. They maintain contact with friends and collaborators from many phases of their lives, people whose political beliefs range from varying shades of socialism and anarchism to the ideology of the Tea Party (to the extent that it has a coherent ideology). They remain close with comrades from the Workers Solidarity Club, with steelworkers Ed Mann and John Barbero; with Sami Bahour and other Palestinian activists; and with inmates Keith LaMar, Jason Robb, and George Skatzes. Of course, the struggles of some of these men and women are far from over; LaMar and Robb, for example, remain inmates at the Ohio State Penitentiary in Youngstown.

These friends have great respect for the Lynds' work—and for their energy. "I'm fifty," commented Jim Jordan, a former steelworker and longtime friend and collaborator, "and I know that I couldn't keep up with [Staughton] and Alice. My wife is intimidated by them. She says, 'They're very nice, but they make you feel so inefficient. Like you never do anything for anybody.'"[1] Another friend and comrade is Todd Gitlin, a former SDS leader turned academic. He remarked that during the late

The audience listens with rapt attention to Staughton's address, given 20 March 2007. Kent State University Libraries. Special Collections and Archives.

1960s, when much of the New Left was moving away from the communitarian spirit of the civil rights movement to a more doctrinaire worldview, Staughton "was a strong voice for militant nonviolence, the most mature exemplar of that position."[2]

Jim Callen, a lawyer who worked with Staughton at Northeast Ohio Legal Services, reflected on his role in efforts to fight the closing of the steel mills in Youngstown. Even though, as Callen put it, "this idea to get community ownership of the mills really wasn't his idea," much of the criticism of the plan focused on Staughton: "He was a lightning rod for some of the critics." Callen pointed out that the idea for a worker- and community-owned mill came from the Ecumenical Coalition but added that since most of the community leaders that composed it were clergy, "they weren't as easy targets." However, he concluded, "while there were people who attacked Staughton, those who worked with and knew him understood they were dealing with a pretty extraordinary individual."[3]

Eric O'Neill and Lorry Swain are also longtime friends of the Lynds. Eric has worked with Alice and Staughton on labor issues, while Lorry is a longtime prisoners' rights activist. In August 2013, the authors met with the couple at their homestead in northern Kentucky. Lorry expressed her admiration for the Lynds, especially Alice, remarking that she didn't know how Alice and Staughton "keep going like they do—especially Alice." She described Alice and Staughton as true partners. Even though the articulate Staughton often speaks for both of them, she explained, they are true partners because Alice's skills with details, listening, and organization complement Staughton's erudition and powers of argument.[4]

A final reflection on Staughton was provided by Alexis Buss, who is associated with Bindlestiff Books in Philadelphia. The bookstore handles books on labor, socialism, feminism, and anarcho-syndicalism. From 2000 to 2005, Buss was secretary-treasurer of the IWW. In this capacity, she invited Staughton to address the organization's 2005 Centennial Conference. At that conference, she recalled, Staughton's ideas on solidarity unionism and accompaniment helped to "crystalize for me the central tenets of radical labor." She added that it was because of Staughton that she learned of the ideas of Marty Glaberman and Stan Weir concerning workers and self-organization. She concluded by saying that Staughton helped to "bring Wobbly [IWW] ideas up to date."[5]

One of Alice's and Staughton's closest friends was the late historian and political scientist Howard Zinn, who died in 2010. In his introduction to Carl Mirra's biography of Staughton, Zinn wrote that "he and Alice are the exemplar of strength and gentleness in the quest for a better world."[6] With the publication of the first biography of Zinn, *Howard Zinn: A Life on The Left* by Martin Duberman, pundits and academics began a "reevaluation" of the life of Zinn, former shipyard worker, bombardier aviator, civil rights worker, historian, and activist. Alice and Staughton knew Zinn from their days in Atlanta, when Staughton and Howard taught history at Spelman College. When historian David Greenberg, in a review of Duberman's biography, wrote a scathing attack on Zinn, Staughton, Robert Cohen, and Jesse Lemisch wrote responses defending their late friend.[7] On 9 April 2010, at the 2010 conference of the Organization of American Historians, Staughton delivered a moving tribute to Zinn to a session entitled "Remembering Howard Zinn."[8]

Staughton remarked to one of the authors that a long-time friend who had been an SDS leader in the 1960s had later abandoned the radical vision of a better world that they had once shared. He then added that, politics aside, this former comrade would always be his friend. Both Alice and Staughton collaborated with and helped workers and inmates who were politically conservative, who had joined the Aryan Brotherhood in prison, or whose views on the wars in Iraq and Afghanistan were contrary to the Lynds' own. They saw in these people sparks of goodness even though they had embraced political positions that the Lynds could not support. The willingness of Alice and Staughton to reach out and work alongside men and women with whom they disagreed demonstrates their commitment to the principle of accompaniment, but it also illuminates their sense of tolerance and their commitment to the values of "inner light" Quakerism. They did not exhibit the sectarianism and "error knows no right" attitude often found on the American left.

The Detractors Speak

Staughton and Alice had their share of opponents and critics, although Staughton had more than Alice because he wrote more and took more public positions that would open him to criticism. However, neither Alice nor Staughton ever (in our investigation) took positions or changed positions on issues because of external pressure or for material gain. Speaking of Staughton, Jack Walsh, a former shop steward in a Youngstown bakery, commented: "He's not self-motivated. He's not interested in doing it for money. I watched him get out of my car one day and climb over a thirty-inch snow bank to walk a picket line at Youngstown Buick. How many other attorneys you know would do that?"[9] These sentiments were echoed by Tony Budak, whom the authors interviewed on 14 January 2011.

Much of the criticism leveled against Staughton (and much less frequently against Alice) reduces to three basic charges:

1. The Lynds are Communists. This charge has been made against Staughton all his adult life. There are usually two motivations behind the charge. The first is ignorance about just what a Communist is. Both Lynds have embraced a kind of nonideological socialism but neither ever joined a communist organization of any kind. They were never supporters of the Soviet Union, China, or Cuba. While they have admired some features of those countries (especially their health

Tony Budak, foreground, was a longtime tow-motor driver at Packard Electric Plant in Trumbull County, Ohio. Kent State University Libraries. Special Collections and Archives.

care and literacy campaigns) they have always been willing to criticize them for suppression of human rights. The second motivation in making the charge is to smear and discredit the Lynds. In these cases, the critics are not interested in whether the charges are true or not; they simply want to damage the Lynds' reputations. As noted earlier, some critics of the plan to create a worker- and community-owned steel mill leveled this charge at Staughton even though the idea of a publicly owned mill did not originate with him.

2. Staughton and Alice are rank-and-file troublemakers. Staughton's association with rank-and-file movements often prompted this attack, since those movements frequently opposed the entrenched union leaders on either the national or local level. Indeed, Staughton did associate with militant local unionists such as Ed Mann, John Barbero, and Bill Litch. This was the reason he was fired from Youngstown's leading law firm in the area of labor law. Pressure from union leaders, whose locals were clients of the firm, prompted it to terminate

Staughton's employment. After Staughton was fired, Alice continued to work at the firm as a paralegal until pressure from local union leaders prompted it to fire Alice as well. In that instance, Alice had done nothing to provoke the attack; her only fault was being married to Staughton. Lloyd McBride, then president of Steelworkers International, was suspicious of the fact that Staughton had been associated, however loosely, with Ed Sadlowski's 1976–77 insurgent campaign challenging McBride for the union presidency.

3. Staughton and Alice are radical gadflies. This line of criticism contends that Staughton and Alice, with their advanced degrees in law, have tended to meddle in enterprises of which they have little direct knowledge or experience. Of course, those making this charge are not the rank-and-file workers or prisoners who have benefited from the dedicated service provided by the Lynds. These critics tend to be those who were benefiting, directly or indirectly, from the marginalization of these groups and who disliked finding themselves pitted against people newly empowered by the legal expertise of Alice and Staughton. One such critic, Frank Valenta, director of Steelworkers District 28, charged that Staughton "passes himself off as an American steel industry expert, when he knows little or nothing about what is really going on."[10] Others felt that Staughton and his collaborators in the Ecumenical Coalition had raised the hopes of steelworkers and their families only to see them dashed. The problem with both of these criticisms is that they are based on a different conception of trade unionism than that of Alice and Staughton. When confronted with the announcement that the steel mills were closing, Frank Valenta and Lloyd McBride, like most officials of the established unions, took the view that closure was inevitable and that the only course open to works and their unions is not fighting back but rather accepting the closing of the mills while negotiating the best possible terms of surrender. Their criticism of the Lynds reflects this view. Such criticism also blames the Lynds for the radicalism of the groups they sought to help, while failing to acknowledge that the workers or prisoners were radicalized by their own situations. Staughton did not instill militancy in the minds of people like Ed Mann or John Barbero. Both of these men, and many others, were rank-and-file militants *before* Staughton and Alice came along. They were already opposed to the 1973 Experimental

Negotiating Agreement negotiated by McBride's predecessor, I. W. Abel. The Lynds merely walked with these men and women and offered their expertise: a knowledge of the law.

With the common charges leveled against the Lynds debunked and put into context, it might be useful to revisit the principles that actually did motivate their work, principles that have constituted the two major intellectual contributions made by Alice and Staughton during their years in Ohio: accompaniment and solidarity unionism.

Accompaniment

When the Lynds moved to Youngstown in 1976, they had not yet fully evolved the principle of accompaniment, let alone worked out strategies for implementing it. In fact, as Staughton later recalled, "Alice and I had a conversation about when we developed the idea of accompaniment, and to my surprise, we think it was later than I would have supposed because our oldest daughter's son, our grandson, was born in 1987 in London. I remember lying on the bed reading Gustavo Gutiérrez on the preferential option for the poor, so it had to be later than that."[11] Alice added that they may have fully developed the principle even later.

The ideal of accompaniment first began to coalesce for the Lynds when, through the writings of Archbishop Romero and Gustavo Gutiérrez (a Peruvian-born Dominican priest and theologian now on teaching at the University of Notre Dame), they learned of actual experiments in working with marginalized groups in Latin America. Their own experiences in Latin America then consolidated their thinking.

But just what does accompaniment accomplish for the middle-class radical imbued with a socialist consciousness, who wants to influence workers? "The radical movement has forever agonized with the following," Staughton explained. "'How are we going to relate to workers?' 'What should we put in the leaflet tomorrow morning?' I just think that this is such an unsatisfactory way of resolving the dilemma. If you just take the trouble to acquire a skill that is useful to people, I don't think that lawyering is the most important. It might be being a nurse, or being an agronomist, or so many different kinds of things, but it's just extraordinary the degree to which obstacles can then be overcome."[12]

The acquisition of a useful skill enables the radical to get in the front door and eventually to win the confidence of the population he or she seeks to help: workers, the unemployed, retirees, or whatever the group is. However, two problems might surface in using this approach.

The first problem might be called "ultimate goal versus immediate need." The middle-class radical is able to win the confidence of, say, a group of workers because as a lawyer, for example, he or she is able to suggest legal strategies and name cases that are completely outside the experience of the rank-and-file worker. The radical lawyer then becomes deeply involved in the efforts of the group of workers to win control of a union local or to organize a plant. These struggles are critically important without even considering the larger goal of educating workers about and stimulating their interest in basic social change. As the radical becomes ever more immersed in the vital immediate struggles of workers, prisoners or whomever, how and when does he or she reach longer-term goals and the true nature of the struggle? Admittedly, socialism is not something one can offer workers on a take-it-or-leave-it basis, but what is the connection between the immediate struggles and the greater goal?

The second problem could be called "accompaniment as a visible strategy." The authors interviewed many people who have been associated with Alice and Staughton in struggles concerning steel mill closings, violations of civil liberties, prison reform, and other issues. None of these collaborators and friends of the Lynds ever mentioned the word *accompaniment.* While all of them expressed their admiration for the Lynds in terms of their commitment, honesty, openness, and incorruptibility, none ever commented on their use of accompaniment as a strategy for working with people. Why was that? Did these people understand the concept by another name? Did they perhaps feel that by naming accompaniment as a strategy they would be implying that the Lynds were using the workers to advance socialism, addressing short-term struggles only in order to demonstrate the importance of longer-term goals and fundamental social change?

Such questions are particularly interesting because in his book on the subject, *Accompanying,* Staughton skillfully outlines the principle and then distinguishes it from types of labor or community organizing that have been used with mixed results. He explains that one of the distinguishing features of accompaniment is a long-term commitment to working with people to address problems in a community by offering them tangible skills. If accompaniment is to be seen as a viable alternative to some of the traditional approaches to organizing, then it must function as a coherent collection of ideas that can be used and adapted to local situations and struggles. It should not be seen as a catechism but rather as a methodology with enough visibility that people unconnected with the Lynds and unfamiliar with the teachings of Archbishop Romero will want to explore it.

Staughton has stated that the Lynds' principle contribution to the theory and practice of accompaniment is the idea that the radical organizer must live among the people and offer them a concrete skill or set of skills that will help define the relationship between the organizer and the people. Alice adds that her notion of "the two experts," which she formulated long ago while she was doing draft counseling work, became an important part of accompaniment, especially in working with prisoners. The key element for Alice was acknowledging that the prisoner (like the young man facing the draft) was an expert on his life and that listening to the prisoner describe his life validates for the prisoner the importance of his experiences.[13]

Solidarity Unionism

The efforts of Staughton and Alice on behalf of workers and the labor movement since their move to Youngstown in 1976 have drawn on a wealth of experiences from earlier in their lives, including their involvement in the Writers' Workshop in Gary, Indiana, between 1969 and 1971 and in the Sadlowski campaign in 1973 and their associations with rank-and-file activists like Ed Mann and John Barbero, whose friendship was part of the reason they chose to move to Youngstown. Once settled there, their activism found many outlets: work for the city's most important labor law firm; the fight against the steel mill shutdowns in the Mahoning Valley; involvement in the Workers Solidarity Club, Solidarity USA, and WATCH; and their work with nurses and health aides of the Visiting Nurses Association who wished to organize. All of these experiences helped the Lynds formulate and refine the principle of solidarity unionism.

There is no doubt that both Alice and Staughton have had negative experiences in dealing with the leaders of some unions—leaders like Lloyd McBride of the Steelworkers. McBride's hostility to the idea of a worker-owned steel mill in Youngstown was a deep disappointment to the Lynds, as well as to those in and around the Ecumenical Coalition who had promoted and lobbied for it. Yet such negative experiences contributed to the development of solidarity unionism.

This brand of unionism has several important characteristics. First, it promotes *horizontal relationships* rather than hierarchical ones. Unions under this model would develop fraternal cooperative relationships with other unions in a plant, or neighborhood, or city. This stands in sharp contrast to the governing philosophy of most unions, where the power flows down from the international through *vertical* relationships with regions and locals. Second, it relies on *voluntarism,* maximizing rank-and-file control through voluntary participation in union-sponsored events and political action and the direct payment of dues. Third, it safeguards *minority representation.* In the United States, representation is usually arranged so that the winner takes all. This is true of our political system and it also predominates in labor and industrial relations. If two unions compete for bargaining rights in a representation election, for example, the results might be as follows:

Representation	Percentage of Vote
Union A	51%
Union B	42%
No Union	7%

Under our current system, this would mean that Union A would represent 100 percent of the workers while holding only 51 percent of the vote. The union with 42 percent of the vote would get nothing. Solidarity unionism envisions the possibility of minority representation or even of a confederation type of bargaining with the two strongest unions participating. The fourth and last characteristic of solidarity unionism is *rank-and-file control.* This emphasis on local control would provide for the reempowerment of the shop steward and seek to settle potential grievances on the shop floor with the workers involved rather than through a long-drawn-out procedure where the union owns the grievance and settles it without consulting the grievant. This model would also reject so called management rights prerogatives and oppose no-strike provisions during the life of the contract.

Concerns with Solidarity Unionism

The attitude of national unions toward worker-owned cooperatives has changed. In his book, *What Then Must We Do? Straight Talk about the Next American Revolution,* Gar Alperovitz points out that while the Steelworkers Union under McBride opposed the Youngstown effort to start a worker- and community-owned cooperative steel mill, the same union now supports the idea. According to Alperovitz, "The United Steelworkers, whose national leadership once opposed the Youngstown effort, has also evolved. The union recently announced a major strategy to help build 'union co-op' worker-owned companies around the nation. Efforts are under way, in particular, in Pittsburgh and Cincinnati."[14]

In some respects, the model(s) of solidarity unionism are hostile to the current organization of the labor movement in the United States. In particular, the concept is counter-posed to the current reality of bureaucratic, international unions headquartered in Washington, D.C., and run in a consistently top-down fashion. If the labor movement were to devolve into a federation of local unions, therefore, how much political influence and of what kind would it wield on the legislative process in Washington? While we all like to emphasize the importance of the Southern civil rights movement and the work of Dr. King, Clarence Mitchell, the late lobbyist of the NAACP, admitted that without the efforts of the AFL-CIO leadership, notably Andrew Biemiller, on Capitol Hill, the 1964 Civil Rights Act and 1965 Voting Rights Act would not have been enacted.

Finally, the two Youngstown-area groups practicing solidarity unionism that Staughton cited in his book *Solidarity Unionism*, the Workers Solidarity Club and Solidarity USA, neither remains today, while the union of nurses formed by the Visiting Nurses Association is today affiliated with SEIU. Why did this occur? Staughton addressed this very issue in a conversation with the authors:

> So the fact of the matter is whether you look at Visiting Nurses, Solidarity . . . these were all remarkable experiences, but none of them

became permanent organizations. It brings to mind a book by Frances Fox Piven and Richard Cloward called *Poor People's Movements*, in which they argue that whether you look at trade unionism or the later welfare rights movement . . . the period of time in which all these movements really accomplished something is before they were institutionalized, when they took the form of networks of people who were taking direct action and were relating horizontally to one another. After the unions were formed, collective bargaining [was] entered into with a no-strike clause. You just didn't have the same degree of success, even from a material point of view, as was achieved in the primitive, unorganized phase.[15]

The last part of this statement by Staughton represents a considerable generalization about the formation of the first industrial unions in the United States in the 1920s and 1930s. Certainly the experiences of a John Sargent or a Stan Weir must be considered. However, are workers' self-organization efforts before the arrival of a union always more vital and democratic? Why are there not more examples of solidarity unionism around the country, other than the IWW's effort to organize baristas at Starbucks and low-wage workers in chain retail stores?

The Youngstown Steel Mills

The effort to save the mills, and the Lynds' involvement in it, has already been discussed at length. It only remains to comment that this struggle was path-breaking in terms of the precedent it set. Alperovitz points out that while the effort didn't save Youngstown's steel mills, its idea of community ownership led to successful struggles elsewhere: out of the "Youngstown idea" came a decentralized movement for worker-owned businesses in Ohio and throughout the country.[16] Today, worker-owned businesses, co-ops, and publicly owned services are burgeoning in local communities across the United States. Although the idea was not his, Staughton played an important role in fostering it in Youngstown. Perhaps the idea began when trade unionist Gerald Dickey asked, "Why don't we just buy the damn thing?" Perhaps Dickey was saying what others were also thinking. The point is that the idea for a worker- and community-owned mill came from a worker, or perhaps several workers. It was not handed down by officials in Pittsburgh (headquarters of the USW leadership) or in Washington, D.C. (the Carter administration). Staughton helped this grassroots idea grow.

Prison Work

One has only to read Michelle Alexander's 2011 book, *The New Jim Crow: Mass Incarceration in an Age of Color-Blindness,* to appreciate the rise of a kind of prison culture in the United States. Alice and Staughton became involved in prison issues in the early 1990s. They opposed the building of the supermax prison in Youngstown, and, together with attorneys like Jules Lobel and Niki Schwartz, they initiated lawsuits on behalf of the inmates who were convicted of leading the 1993 Lucasville prison rebellion and sentenced to death. In talks with the authors, two of the Lucasville Five have praised the Lynds' the tireless work on their behalf and acknowledged the difference it has made in the quality of their living conditions in prison. Both also recalled how the Lynds included the inmates in discussions that would affect their lives and spoke about the "different kind of lawyers" that Alice and Staughton were. In line with the principal of accompaniment, the Lynds "walked with" the inmates.

During their years in Ohio, the Lynds worked alongside workers in the Mahoning Valley to try to create a worker- and community-owned steel mill as a way to provide employment for at least some of the thousands of steelworkers who lost their jobs when the parent companies closed the mills. They have also worked to improve prison conditions and to broaden the civil rights of inmates in solitary confinement in Ohio's prisons. Furthermore, the Lynds' commitment to participatory democracy and self-organization prompted Staughton to develop the concept of solidarity unionism, based on building horizontal connections between workers and their unions and among workers belonging to different unions in an effort to restore at least some democracy to the labor movement. The values of accompaniment helped the Lynds to build these efforts in ways that included the workers or the prisoners themselves. They sought to work *with* rather than *for* workers and prisoners in their struggles, refusing to follow the usual approach of cutting a deal on their behalf behind closed doors and then delivering the results to them as a kind of fait accompli. Accompaniment is the source of the values of participation and community that have made the contributions of the Lynds unique.

Over the course of their lives, the Lynds have directed their activism into a range of channels while consistently practicing their ideals. Much of their work was done for very little money and some of it was done on a volunteer basis. Today Alice and Staughton still live simply in the house they bought in 1976 and in which they raised their youngest child. Still walking side by side, they remain vitally interested in improving their world, engaged with their friends and fellow workers, and active in many struggles.

Chapter Thirteen ⟞⟝

FINAL WORDS

"Anything we do together is better than anything we
could do separately."

ALICE LYND

Guatemala

In July 2013, the authors journeyed to the house on Timbers Court to
meet with Martha Lynd Altan, daughter of Alice and Staughton Lynd.
Martha lives with her husband and son in a Mayan village near Lake
Atitlan in Guatemala, about a four-hour journey from Guatemala
City. She had returned her childhood home in Niles, Ohio, for a brief
visit to celebrate her mother's eighty-third birthday.

Martha is the youngest child of Alice and Staughton, following Barbara Lynd Bond, a Catholic school teacher in the Youngstown area, and
Lee Lynd, a professor at Dartmouth. While all three of the Lynd children
have pursued the values of their parents in one way or another, Martha seems to have come closest to practicing the principle of accompaniment that has defined the lives of her parents for several decades.
She works with Mayan women in her community who are backstrap
weavers and who need the money that might come from marketing
their goods to people in the United States and Canada. Through the
Traditional Mayan Foundation, Martha helps the women weavers to
sell what they make.[1]

Health and Belief

In 2007, Staughton entered the hospital. Pictures obtained from a heart
catheterization showed an almost complete blockage of the flow of

blood to his heart. The doctors performed a triple bypass operation. For six weeks, Staughton could not drive. Since Alice does not drive, daughter Barbara picked up prescriptions for her father as he recuperated at home. Both the doctor and Barbara told him that God had spared him for a reason.[2]

Alice and Staughton have stated that they do not believe in a supernatural deity, yet on some occasions, they refer to themselves as Quakers, implying a belief in some Quaker practices and values, such as nonviolence. There is a network of nontheistic Quakers in the United States.

The issue of religion, raised by Barbara and the doctor during Staughton's health crisis, is important because it helps us to examine the Lynds' links with various religious and secular peace traditions. In their willingness to engage in nonviolent direct action and individual or collective moral witness, Alice and Staughton are close to the tradition of the pacifist Left represented by nonviolent activists such as A. J. Muste (1885–1967), David Dellinger (1915–2004), and David McReynolds. Both Alice and Staughton believe strongly in nonviolence as essential in forging a better world. Staughton refers to himself as a socialist, while Alice has said during several interviews and conversations that while she may identify with some of the values of the American Left, she is not a leftist.

So where does that leave us? It is conventional among many on the left to seek to place individual activists somewhere along the continuum from mere reform to outright revolution. This kind of oversimplification does not work in the case of Alice and Staughton. Rather, we must see their positions as matters of scale. Staughton is not calling for an overthrow of the government, but neither is he satisfied with tinkering with the machinery at the top, which is what most reforms end up being. Rather, Staughton has called for radical local experiments in cooperative or worker-owned management of businesses and services. Writing about the Youngstown experiences, Staughton made the following observation in *The Fight Against Shutdowns:* "What was new in the Youngstown venture was the notion that workers and community residents could own and operate a *steel mill* . . . Employee-community ownership of the Campbell Works would have challenged the capitalist system on the terrain of large-scale enterprises in basic industries . . . This was the ownership model the workers chose."[3]

Legacy

We owe the Lynds a debt of gratitude.

Through their work as lawyers, historians, and activists, they have helped to expand our notion of democracy in American life. Democracy is not something that happens only in the voting booth. It should not end at the door of the shop or workplace, where the right of the employer to control both property and labor—that is, human beings—trumps any notion of democracy. Both Alice and Staughton have challenged this cramped view of democracy. Both of them speak and act on the belief that democracy should extend to almost every facet of life.[4]

Through the Macedonia experience, through the civil rights movement, through draft counseling and their advocacy of small-scale lo-

Staughton and Alice Lynd posed for this December 2003 portrait in a friend's kitchen. Kent State University Libraries. Special Collections and Archives.

cal change, Alice and Staughton have taught us a fundamental lesson: Perhaps we should realize that a better world doesn't always have to be a particular *type* of society. It can also be a process . . . a way of living, a collective exercise in self-definition and self-governance.[5] A movement that defines itself by how decisions are made and by how people treat one another can start to prefigure a new society, the "better world" about which we so often talk but that we never quite know how to reach.

With these observations, our story ends. Alice and Staughton continue their work according to their health and energy. They have given us two important intellectual legacies. In accompaniment, they have given us the idea that the radical comes to a community and offers the people a set of practical skills/knowledge that they need. In this way, the radical organizer becomes part of a struggle not because of ideological conviction but because of the skills or knowledge that she or he brings to it. Their second legacy, solidarity unionism, is an expression of applied accompaniment, which they employed in their work with steel workers, health workers, and prisoners. They have taught us, through speech, writing, and example, about change from the bottom up rather than the top down. They have helped people in many struggles, from steelworkers to autoworkers, from health workers to Nicaraguan villagers, from the dispossessed in Israel/Palestine to the Lucasville Five. In the conclusion of *Stepping Stones,* Alice invites us on a journey: "This book invites you to take a journey with us. Perhaps you will see some possibility that did not occur to us, or otherwise feel strengthened in finding your own way."[6] We hope that the readers of this slender volume will take Alice up on her invitation. The radical promise for which many of us hope is not always a destination: it may instead be a journey, a journey made side by side.

NOTES

Introduction and Acknowledgments

1. Alice Lynd and Stoughton Lynd, *Stepping Stones: Memoir of a Life Together* (Lanham, Md.: Lexington Books, 2009), 19.

2. See Oscar Romero, *Voice of the Voiceless: Four Pastoral Letters and Other Statements* (Maryknoll, N.Y.: Orbis Books, 1985).

3. See Carl Mirra, *The Admirable Radical: Staughton Lynd and Cold War Dissent, 1945–1970* (Kent, Ohio: Kent State Univ. Press, 2010).

1. Burnham's Dilemma

1. Mary-Alice Waters, ed., *Rosa Luxemburg Speaks* (New York: Pathfinder Press, 1970).

2. See Paul Avrich, "What is 'Makhaevism'?" *Soviet Studies* 17 (July 1965): 1:66, reproduced at http://libcom.org/history/what-makhaevism-paul-avrich. Paul Avrich (1931–2006) did much of the first scholarly work on Jan Waclaw Machajski.

3. See Waclaw Machajaski [*sic*], "On the Expropriation of the Capitalists," in *The Making of Society*, ed. V. F. Calverton (New York: Modern Library, 1937), 427–36. This chapter consists of three excerpts from parts 1 and 3 of Machajski's masterwork, *The Intellectual Worker*, a collection of essays published in Geneva in 1905 as *Umstvennyi rabochii.*

4. Schachtman and Burnham left the Socialist Workers Party in 1939. In a review of *The Managerial Revolution* by James Burnham, Joseph Hansen, another member of the SWP, accused Burnham of taking his ideas, without attribution, from an earlier book by Bruno Rizzi, *The Bureaucratization of the World* (New York: Free Press, 1945). For a sympathetic treatment of James Burnham, especially in his later conservative phase, please see *James Burnham and the Struggle for the World* by Daniel P. Kelly (Wilmington, Del.: ISI Books, 2002).

5. S. Lynd, "Edward Thompson's Warrens," in *From Here to There: The Staughton Lynd Reader*, ed. Andrej Grubacic (Oakland, Calif.: PM Press, 2010), 28. A short discussion of the impact of Thompson's *The Making of the English Working Class* on American labor history is found in *The Age of Fracture* by Daniel T. Rodgers (Cambridge, Mass.: Belknap Press, 2011), 91–97.

6. E. P. Thompson, "At the Point of Decay," in *Out of Apathy*, ed. E. P. Thompson (London: Stevens, 1960), 6.

7. For a discussion of the secret funding of the Congress for Cultural Freedom (CCF) by the United States Central Intelligence Agency (CIA), please see James Petras's review of Frances Stonor Saunders's *Who Paid the Piper: The CIA and the Cultural Cold War*, "The CIA and the Cultural Cold War Revisited," *Monthly Review* 51, no. 6 (Nov. 1999), 47–66. See also Peter Coleman's history of the CCF, *The Liberal Conspiracy* (New York: Free Press, 1989).

8. S. Lynd, "The First New Left . . . and the Third," chapter 5 of his *Living Inside Our Hope: A Steadfast Radical's Thoughts on Rebuilding the Movement* (Ithaca, N.Y.: ILR Press paperback, Cornell Univ. Press, 1997), 67–88.

9. See Michael Wiezin, *Rebel in Defense of Tradition: The Life and Politics of Dwight Macdonald* (New York: Basic Books, 1994).

10. See S. Lynd: *Living Inside Our Hope*, 68–69; and Alexander Stille's foreword to *The Abruzzo Trilogy: Fontamara, Bread and Wine, and Seed Beneath the Snow* by Ignazio Silone (Steerforth, Vt.: Steerforth Press, 2000), vii–viii.

11. See John Foot, "The Secret Life of Ignazio Silone," *New Left Review* 3 (May–June 2000), reproduced at the journal's website, http://www.newleftreview.org/?page=article&review+2250.

12. A. Lynd and S. Lynd, *Stepping Stones*, 93.

2. Draft Counseling as Accompaniment

1. A. Lynd and S. Lynd, *Stepping Stones*, 84–85.

2. Ibid., 85.

3. Ibid., 85.

4. For an account of Lynd's dismissal from Yale University, see Mirra, *The Admirable Radical*, 117–49.

5. A. Lynd and S. Lynd, interview by authors, 9 Nov. 2009, Niles, Ohio.

6. Ibid.

7. Ibid. For an account of the Lynd's life at the Macedonia Cooperative Community, please see A. Lynd and S. Lynd, *Stepping Stones*, 45–59. For a book-length study, see Edward Orser, *Searching for a Viable Alternative: The Macedonia Cooperative Community, 1937–1958* (New York: Lenox Hill Publishers, 1982).

8. A. Lynd and S. Lynd, interview by authors, 9 Nov. 2009, Niles, Ohio.

3. Oral History from Below

1. A. Lynd and S. Lynd, interview by authors, 9 Nov. 2009, Niles, Ohio.

2. For an example of this kind of analysis, see Peter Collier and David Horowitz, *Destructive Generation: Second Thoughts About the Sixties* (1989: New York: Free Press, 1996); and Eugene D. Genovese, "The Question," *Dissent* (Summer 1994): 377–88.

3. In January 2010, Staughton Lynd acknowledged a debt to Zinn for the use of oral history in a letter to Michael Honey at the History News Network, "Remembering Howard Zinn," reproduced on the website of Rich Gibson,

emeritus professor of social studies at San Diego State University. See the text of the letter linked to Rich Gibson's Education Page for Eguality, Justice, Freedom, and Retribution at http://richgibson.com/RememberingHowardZinn. html.

4. See, for example, Jesse Lemisch, "The American Revolution Seen from the Bottom Up," in *Towards a New Past: Dissenting Essays in American History*, ed. Barton J. Bernstein (New York: Pantheon Books, 1968); Howard Zinn, *The Politics of History* (Boston, Mass.: Beacon Press, 1970); S. Lynd, "Oral History from Below," *Oral History Review* 21 (Spring 1993): 3.

5. Ed Wells, interview by authors, 8 Apr. 2011, Youngstown, Ohio.

6. S. Lynd, "Oral History from Below, *Oral History Review* 21, no. 1 (Spring 1993): 2.

7. Ibid., 2–5.

4. The View from the Shop Floor

1. A. Lynd and S. Lynd, interviewed by authors, 9 Nov. 2009, Niles, Ohio.

2. A. Lynd and S. Lynd, interviewed by authors, 20 Apr. 2010, Niles, Ohio.

3. Gary, Indiana, Writers' Workshop and S. Lynd, *Two Steel Contracts* (Boston, Mass.: New England Free Press, 1971). Reprinted from the Sept.–Oct. 1971 edition of *Radical America.*

4. Ibid., 2.

5. S. Lynd, *Accompanying: Pathways to Social Change* (Oakland, Calif.: PM Press, 2012), 24.

6. Ibid., 24–25.

7. An excellent account of the events leading to the unseating of the delegates from the Mississippi Freedom Democratic Party at the 1964 Democratic Party can be found in Taylor Branch's book *Pillar of Fire: America in the King Years, 1963–65* (New York: Simon and Schuster, 1999).

8. A. Lynd and S. Lynd, interview by authors, 15 Jan. 2011, Niles, Ohio.

9. University-educated Martin Glaberman was employed as an autoworker for more than twenty years. He was associated with C. L. R. James (1901–1989), a West Indian socialist and advocate of workers' self-activity. Staughton Lynd has introduced and edited a collection of the writings of Martin Glaberman, including the pamphlet *Punching Out*, in Martin Glaberman, *Punching Out and Other Writings*, ed. Staughton Lynd (Chicago, Ill.: Charles H. Kerr, 2002). For more information on James, see Ken Worcester's book, *C. L. R. James: A Political Biography* (New York: State Univ. of New York Press, 1996).

10. S. Lynd, "Speech Before the IWW Centennial Convention," in *From Here To There*, ed. Andrej Grubacic (Oakland, Calif.: PM Press, 2010), 243.

11. A. Lynd and S. Lynd, interview by authors, 15 Jan. 2011, Niles, Ohio.

12. See Steve Early, *Civil Wars in U.S. Labor : Birth of a New Workers' Movement or Death Throes of the Old?* (Chicago, Ill.: Haymarket Books, 2010).

13. See Don Stillman, *Stronger Together: The Story of SEIU* (White River Junction, Vt.: Chelsea Green, 2010).

14. See C. Wright Mills, *New Men of Power: America's Labor Leaders* (1948; Champaign: Univ. of Illinois Press, 2001).

15. Stillman, *Stronger Together,* 36.

16. See Cal Winslow, *Labor's Civil War in California: The NUHW Health-care Workers' Rebellion* (Oakland, Calif.: PM Press, 2010).

17. A. Lynd and S. Lynd, interview by authors, 18 May 2010, Niles, Ohio.

18. A. Lynd and S. Lynd, interview by authors, 20 Apr. 2010, Niles, Ohio. The group Facing Reality came out of the Johnson-Forest Tendency, a group led by C. L. R. James and Raya Dunayevskaya. The Johnson-Forest Tendency had come out of the Socialist Workers Party in 1951, breaking with the SWP because of the former's analysis that the Soviet Union was "state capitalist." In the early 1950s, James was forced to leave the United States for Britain. The Johnson-Forest Tendency changed its name to the Correspondence Publishing Committee, which itself split into two groups. One group remained loyal to James and retained the name Correspondence Publishing Committee. The other group, which was loyal to Raya Dunayevskaya, became the News and Letters Committee; it remains in existence today and publishes a monthly newspaper entitled *News and Letters.*

19. According to Staughton Lynd, the term *contractualism* was first used by Ed Mann (1928–1992).

20. A. Lynd and S. Lynd, interview by authors, 20 April 2010, Niles, Ohio.

21. S. Lynd, A. Lynd, and Manny Ness, "Forging Rank-and-File Solidarity Unionism Today: A Roundtable Discussion" (paper presented at the United Association for Labor Education Annual Conference, Pittsburgh, Pa., 22 Mar. 2012).

22. Frank Bardacke, *Trampling Out the Vintage: Cesar Chavez and the Two Souls of the United Farmworkers* (London: Verso, 2011). Other recent studies include Miriam Pawel, *The Union of Their Dreams: Power, Hope, and Struggle in Cesar Chavez's Farm Worker Movement* (New York: Bloomsbury Press, 2009); and Marshall Ganz, *Why David Sometimes Wins* (New York: Oxford Univ. Press, 2009).

5. Transition—Becoming Lawyers

1. A. Lynd and S. Lynd, *Stepping Stones,* 103.

2. Ibid., 105.

3. Ibid., 106.

4. Ibid., 106.

5. S. Lynd, *The Fight Against Shutdowns: Youngstown's Steel Mill Closings* (San Pedro, Calif.: Singlejack Books, 1982), 6.

6. A. Lynd and S. Lynd, interview by authors, 15 Jan. 2010, Niles, Ohio.

7. A. Lynd and S. Lynd, interview by authors, 9 Nov. 2009, Niles, Ohio.

8. Ibid.

9. Ibid.

10. Ibid.

11. In 1964, a group of third-camp socialists split from the Socialist Party, USA to form the Independent Socialist Clubs of America (ISCA). In 1966, Stan Weir wrote "A New Era of Labor Revolt: On the Job Vs. Official Unions" (New York: Independent Socialist Clubs of America, 1966) as a pamphlet for the ISCA. Another memorable pamphlet, by ISCA leader and Berkeley librarian

Hal Draper, was "Two Souls of Socialism," *New Politics* 5, no.1 (Winter 1966): 57–84. Later, the Independent Socialist Clubs became the International Socialists and then joined with other groups to form Solidarity, a multitendency socialist organization, which publishes *Against the Current*.

12. A. Lynd and S. Lynd, interview by authors, 16 Mar. 2012, Niles, Ohio.

13. Ibid.

14. Fortunately, this fine book has been published in a second edition by PM Press of Oakland, California. See Staughton Lynd and Daniel Gross, *Labor Law for the Rank and Filer: Building Solidarity While Staying Clear of the Law*, 2d ed. (1978; Oakland, Calif.: PM Press, 2011).

15. S. Lynd and Gross, *Labor Law for the Rank and Filer*, 11.

16. Mike Parker and Martha Gruelle, *Democracy is Power: Rebuilding Unions from the Bottom Up* (Detroit, Mich.: Labor Notes, 1999), 96.

17. Julius Getman, *Restoring the Power of Unions: It Takes a Movement* (New Haven, Conn.: Yale Univ. Press, 2010), 11.

18. A. Lynd and S. Lynd, interview by authors, 16 Mar. 2012, Niles, Ohio.

19. Ibid.

20. Ibid.

21. Ibid.

22. A. Lynd and S. Lynd, *Stepping Stones*, 107.

23. Ibid., 110–11.

6. The Fight Against the Shutdowns

1. S. Lynd, *Accompanying*, 28.

2. For more information on Youngstown's steel closures, see S. Lynd, *The Fight Against the Shutdowns*.

3. Ibid., 20–21.

4. This information comes from the Western Reserve Development Agency. It is cited in Thomas G. Fuechtmann, *Steeples and Stacks: Religion and the Steel Crisis in Youngstown* (Cambridge, Mass.: Cambridge Univ. Press, 1989), 15, which is a detailed study of the Ecumenical Coalition of the Mahoning Valley.

5. Youngstown Committee of the Ohio Sesquicentennial Commission, *Industry and Commerce in Youngstown* (Youngstown: N.p., 1953), 22.

6. Fuechtmann, *Steeples and Stacks*, 21.

7. Michael P. Grzesiak, "The Ecumenical Coalition of the Mahoning Valley: How Church Leaders Became Involved in the Steel Business" (M.A. thesis, Department of Philanthropic Studies, Indiana University, May 2008), 12–13. The authors knew Grzesiak when he was a development officer at Kent State University and spent some time servicing the Kent State Library. On the Ecumenical Coalition, see also Roger Wolcott, "The Church and Social Action: Steelworkers and Bishops in Youngstown" (paper presented to the Pennsylvania Sociological Society in Philadelphia, Pa., 3 Nov. 1979, available in M91–219, box 1, folder 1, in Staughton Lynd Papers [hereafter, S. Lynd Papers], State Historical Society of Wisconsin, Madison, Wisc); a version of the paper was published in the *Journal for the Scientific Study of Religion* 21, no. 1 (March 1982).

8. M91–219, box 1, folder 1, S. Lynd Papers.

9. S. Lynd, *The Fight Against Shutdowns*, 23.

10. Ibid., 29. See also S. Lynd, "Worker-Community Ownership in Youngstown," *WIN Magazine*, 25 Jan. 1979, 4–11.

11. See the *Brier Hill Unionist*, Oct.–Nov. 1977.

12. Gar Alperovitz has written widely on the issue of public ownership of businesses. See his article, "Not So Wild a Dream," *The Nation*, 11 June 2012, 18–23. These ideas were also set down in his book, *America Beyond Capitalism: Reclaiming Our Wealth, Our Liberty, and Our Democracy* (Hoboken, N.J.: J. Wiley, 2005). Six years before the steel mill closings in Youngstown, Alperovitz and Staughton Lynd collaborated on a book, *Strategy and Program: Two Essays Toward a New American Socialism* (Boston, Mass.: Beacon Press, 1973).

13. S. Lynd, *The Fight Against Shutdowns*, 34–35.

14. John Sharick, interview by authors, 15 Aug. 2011, Austintown, Ohio.

15. S. Lynd, "The Genesis of the Idea of a Community Right to Industrial Property in Youngstown and Pittsburgh, 1977–1987," *Journal of American History* 74, no. 3 (Dec. 1987): 926–58; reprinted in *Living Inside Our Hope*, ed. S. Lynd (Ithaca, N.Y.: Cornell Univ. Press, 1997), 159–88, quote, 160.

16. S. Lynd, *The Fight Against Shutdowns*, 50.

17. Fuechtmann, *Steeples and Stacks*, 75.

18. The following two books by Robert Weir were helpful in understanding the Knights of Labor and producer cooperatives: *Knights Unhorsed: Internal Conflict in Gilded Age Social Movements* (Detroit, Mich.: Wayne State Univ. Press, 2000); and *Beyond Labor's Veil: The Culture of the Knights of Labor* (Philadelphia: Univ. of Pennsylvania Press, 1996). See also Leon Fink, *Workingmen's Democracy: the Knights of Labor and American Politics* (Champaign: Univ. of Illinois Press, 1983).

19. M91–219, box 2, folder 1, S. Lynd Papers.

20. S. Lynd, *The Fight Against Shutdowns*, 71.

21. M91–219, box 1, folder 3, S. Lynd Papers.

22. Sherry Lee Linkon and John Russo, *Steeltown U.S.A.: Work and Memory in Youngstown* (Lawrence: Univ. of Kansas Press, 2002), 49–50.

23. Ibid., 50.

24. M91–219, box 2, folder 1, S. Lynd Papers.

25. M91–219, box 2, folder 2, S. Lynd Papers.

26. Ibid.

27. S. Lynd, *The Fight Against Shutdowns*, 106–10.

28. Ibid., 111.

29. Ibid., 121–22.

30. Beth Hepfner, interview by authors, 25 Apr. 2011, Niles, Ohio.

31. A. Lynd and S. Lynd, *Stepping Stones*, 107–8.

32. Ibid., 108.

33. Linkon and Russo, *Steeltown U.S.A.*, 232. For quotation within extract, see also Roy R. Weil and Mary H. Shaw, eds., Canoeing Guide: Western Pennsylvania, Northern West Virginia, 7th ed. (Pittsburgh, Pa.: American Youth Hostels, 1983), 92.

34. A. Lynd and S. Lynd, *Stepping Stones,* 108.

35. S. Lynd, "Community Right to Industrial Property," 170–71.

36. James Callen, interview by authors, 15 Aug. 2013, Mineral Ridge, Ohio.

37. S. Lynd, "Community Right to Industrial Property," 173.

38. J. Callen, interview by authors, 15 Aug. 2013, Mineral Ridge, Ohio.

39. S. Lynd, "Community Right to Industrial Property," 174.

7. Solidarity Unionism

1. The Youngstown story is also vividly told in the documentary film *Shout Youngstown* by two women from Youngstown, Dorie Krauss and Carol Greenwald Brouder. See *Shout Youngstown,* produced and directed by Carol Greenwald and Dorie Krauss (New York: Cinema Guild, 1984). It can be obtained from Cinema Guild, Inc., 115 West 30th Street, Suite 800, New York, N.Y., 10001, www.cinemaguild.com.

2. This point about reemployment is made several times by Thomas Fuechtmann in *Steeples and Stacks;* see, for example, 75, 130.

3. See Staughton Lynd, ed., *"We Are All Leaders": The Alternative Unionism of the 1930s* (Champaign: Univ. of Illinois Press, 1966).

4. Archbishop Oscar Romero (1917–1980) was murdered by gunmen in March 1980, while celebrating a mass for poor people in San Salvador. Several individuals have come forward to admit that the assassination was ordered by right-wing politician Roberto d'Aubuisson (1944–1992), who was trained at the School of the Americas in Georgia. D'Aubuisson died of cancer in 1992. He was never tried or even indicted for any of the death squad murders in El Salvador. Romero is often linked to the doctrine called "liberation theology," which actually predated his rise to high church office in El Salvador. Liberation theology was a powerful force not only in Latin America, where it began, but later in the United States. In the United States, often shorn of its Marxist underpinnings, it influenced not only Catholics committed to implementing Catholic social teachings but also secular intellectuals like Harvey Cox and others who saw in it an alternative to intellectual libertarianism popularized by Robert Nozick in his book *Anarchy, The State, and Utopia* (which won the 1975 National Book Award for philosophy).

5. Andrej Grubacic is an anarchist from Yugoslavia, in the Balkan region of Europe. He is coauthor, with Staughton Lynd, of *Wobblies and Zapatistas: Conversations on Anarchism, Marxism, and Radical History* (Oakland, Calif.: PM Press, 2008).

6. See Andrej Grubacic, "Introduction: Libertarian Socialism for the Twenty-First Century," in Staughton Lynd, *From Here to There,* 3–27.

7. S. Lynd, "Toward Another World," in his *From Here to There,* 293.

8. Staughton Lynd, "Rank and File." This is an as yet unpublished manuscript submitted to *New Labor Forum* in June 2012.

9. For a useful discussion of the legal context for minority or "members only" unions, see Charles J. Morris, *The Blue Eagle at Work: Reclaiming Democratic Rights in the American Workplace* (Ithaca, N.Y.: Cornell Univ. Press, 2005).

10. A. Lynd and S. Lynd, interview by authors, 20 April 2010, Niles, Ohio.

11. For a short, informal treatment of the ideas of both Stan Weir and Marty Glaberman, see Steve Early's essay, "Working-Class Intellectuals" in his book, *Embedded With Organized Labor* (New York: Monthly Review Press, 2009), 59–64.

12. See Stan Weir, "The Informal Work Group," in *Rank and File: Personal Histories of Working-Class Organizers*, ed. A. and S. Lynd (Boston, Mass.: Beacon Press, 1973), 179–200.

13. S. Lynd, "From Globalization to Resistance," in his *From Here to There*, 205–18.

14. S. Lynd and Grubacic, *Wobblies and Zapatistas*, 239–40.

15. Andrej Grubacic, introduction to S. Lynd's *From Here to There*, 15.

8. Specific Alternatives to Business Unionism

1. A. Lynd and S. Lynd, *Stepping Stones*, 115. Howard Zinn, a longtime friend of Alice and Staughton, briefly describes the scene in this now-famous photo of Staughton Lynd, David Dellinger, and Bob Moses in his memoir, *You Can't Stay Neutral on a Moving Train: A Personal History of Our Times* (Boston, Mass.: Beacon Press, 1994), 108.

2. S. Lynd, *Solidarity Unionism: Rebuilding the Labor Movement From the Bottom Up* (Chicago, Ill.: Charles H. Kerr, 1992), 15. The Charles H. Kerr Company was founded in 1886, the year of the Haymarket tragedy, by one Charles Hope Kerr, a Unitarian with leanings to the left and to vegetarianism. The company has gone through many stages, developing a close relationship with the Socialist Party and later with a small sect called the Proletarian Party, led by John Keracher. During these years, the Kerr company published the Marxist classics together with the literature of the Proletarian Party, featuring such "classics" as "The Head-Fixing Industry," a pamphlet by John Keracher. Mark knew of the Kerr Company between 1970 and 1975, when its board members included Joe Giganti, Virgil J. Vogel, Fred Thompson, June Kessler, and Burton Rosen. Thompson was a veteran leader of the IWW; while Vogel and Rosen were once associated with an organization called the Libertarian Socialist League. During these years, Mark was state secretary of Socialist Party of Illinois and he had the party's local bulletin printed at the Kerr company. Even after the company's "Proletarian Party phase" ended, one or two members of what remained of the Proletarian Party continued to serve on the Kerr board for a few years.

3. S. Lynd, *Solidarity Unionism*, 15.

4. Ibid.

5. A. Lynd and S. Lynd, *Stepping Stones*, 118.

6. Ibid.

7. Ibid., 119–20.

8. Ibid., 120–21.

9. S. Lynd, *Solidarity Unionism*, 20–21.

10. Quoted in S. Lynd, ed., *Living Inside Our Hope*, 13.

11. See Colin Bossen, "The Chicago Couriers Union, 2003–2010: A Case Study in Solidarity Unionism," *Working USA: A Journal of Labor and Society* 15 (June 2012): 197–215. Bossen edits the "Workers Power" column in the *Industrial Worker.*

12. Ibid., 209–12.

13. Bardacke, *Trampling Out the Vintage,* 67–82. See also Peter Drier, "Rules for Radicals—and Conservatives: The Rightwing World Resurrects Saul Alinsky to Attack Obama," *Jewish Currents* 4 (Summer 2012): 14–19.

14. Bardacke, *Trampling Out the Vintage,* 78.

15. See Daniel Gross and S. Lynd, *Solidarity Unionism at Starbucks* (Oakland, Calif.: PM Press, 2011); pamphlet.

16. Bossen, "Chicago Couriers Union," 212. See also S. Lynd and Gross, *Labor Law for the Rank and Filer.*

17. Bossen, "Chicago Couriers Union," 212–13.

18. The only book-length study of Tony Mazzocchi is Les Leopold's *The Man Who Hated Work and Loved Labor: The Life and Times of Tony Mazzocchi* (White River Junction, Vt.: Chelsea Green Press, 2007).

19. While Staughton gives priority to local organizing, he does not rule out the importance of electoral activity, preferably under the banner of a third party or labor party seeking to address problems either ignored or exacerbated by the two major parties. He also admires the work of earlier labor party formations, such as the United Labor Party, which was active in both Akron and Youngstown.

20. Nelson Lichtenstein, *The Most Dangerous Man in Detroit: Walter Reuther and the Fate of American Labor* (New York: Basic Books, 1995), 434–35.

21. Ibid., *Labor's War at Home: The CIO in World War II* (1982; rev. ed., Philadelphia, Pa.: Temple Univ. Press, 2003), 192–94.

22. See Bardacke, *Trampling Out the Vintage.*

23. Herman Benson, founder of the Association of Union Democracy (AUD) discusses the Sadlowski campaign in his book, *Rebels, Reformers, and Racketeers: How Insurgents Transformed the Labor Movement* (Brooklyn, N.Y.: Association for Union Democracy, 2004), 94–112.

24. David Montgomery, *The Fall of the House of Labor: The Workplace, The State, and American Labor Activism, 1865–1925* (Cambridge, UK: Cambridge Univ. Press, 1987), 317–19.

25. Roy T. Worthman, *From Syndicalism to Trade Unionism: The IWW in Ohio, 1905–1950* (New York: Garland Publishing Co., 1985), 170.

26. Ibid., 176.

27. Fred Thompson wrote "The Workers Who Built Cleveland," which was originally published in the 7 Sept. 1946 issue of *The Industrial Worker* and was reprinted as a pamphlet jointly by the Greater Cleveland Labor History Society and Charles H. Kerr in 1987.

9. Struggle and Solidarity

1. See Carl Mirra, *Citizens and Soldiers: An Oral History of Operation Iraqi Freedom from the Battlefield to the Pentagon* (New York: Palgrave, 2008); see also his *Admirable Radical,* 98–116.

2. See S. Lynd and Thomas Hayden, *The Other Side* (New York: New American Library, 1966).

3. Gail Phares, conversation with Mark W. Weber, 20 Jan. 2012, Bogota, Colombia.

4. A. Lynd and S. Lynd, *Stepping Stones*, 130.

5. Ibid., 133.

6. Ibid., 134.

7. See Staughton Lynd, Sam Bahour, and Alice Lynd, eds., *Homeland: Oral Histories of Palestine and Palestinians* (Ithaca, N.Y.: Olive Branch Press, 1994).

8. For more on such abuses, see the website of Human Rights Watch, http://www.hrw.org/middle-eastn-africa/israel-palestine, and the website of B'Tselem, the Israeli Information Center for Human Rights in the Occupied Territories, http://www.btselem.org.

9. See 2012.3., box 1, Alice and Staughton Lynd Papers, Department of Special Collections and Archives, Kent State University, Kent, Ohio.

10. A. Lynd and S. Lynd, *Stepping Stones*, 138.

11. Ibid.

12. See Shlomo Sand's two books, *The Invention of the Jewish People* (London: Verso, 2009), and *The Invention of the Land of Israel: From Holy Land to Homeland* (London: Verso, 2012).

13. See S. Lynd, Bahour, and A. Lynd, eds., *Homeland*.

14. Jules Lobel, interview by authors, 11 Sept. 2013, Pittsburgh, Pa.

15. Linkon and Russo, *Steeltown U.S.A.*, 53.

16. Ibid., 54.

17. Ibid., 55.

10. Lucasville

1. S. Lynd, "Staughton Lynd, A Personal Letter," *Impact* 8, no. 1 (Apr. 2000): 1, Staughton and Alice Lynd Papers, Department of Special Collections and Archives, Kent State University, Kent, Ohio.

2. Ibid.

3. S. Lynd and A. Lynd, interview by Mark W. Weber, 14 Jan. 2013, Niles, Ohio.

4. The five men constituting the Lucasville Five, of whom three are black and two white, are Keith Lamar, Siddique Abdullah Hasan (Carlos Sanders), Namir Abdul Mateen(James Were), Jason Robb, and George Skatzes. After a riot at a severely overcrowded maximum security prison in Lucasville, Ohio, ended with ten dead, authorities identified the five prisoners named above as ringleaders and held them responsible. All were convicted of aggravated murder and sentenced to death. All five have appeals in various stages of review, with that of Keith Lamar having advanced farthest along the appeals process. Four of the five defendants are being housed at the Ohio prison in Youngstown. George Skatzes, the oldest of the five, is currently being held at the prison in Chillicothe, Ohio.

5. Gary Williams, with Larry Dotson, *Siege in Lucasville: An Insider's Account and Critical Review of Ohio's Worst Prison Riot*, rev. ed. (Bloomington, Ind.: Rooftop Publishers. 2006), vi.

6. A. Lynd and S. Lynd, *Stepping Stones*, 144.

7. Keith Lamar, interview by authors, 18 Sept. 2012, Ohio State Penitentiary, Youngstown, Ohio.

8. Jason Robb, interview by authors, 25 Sept. 2012, Ohio State Penitentiary, Youngstown, Ohio.

9. A. Lynd and S. Lynd, *Stepping Stones*, 145.

10. Keith Lamar, interview by authors, 25 Oct. 2012, Ohio State Penitentiary, Youngstown, Ohio.

11. Jules Lobel, interview by authors, 11 Sept. 2013, Pittsburgh, Pa.

12. The Center for Constitutional Rights was founded in 1966 by attorneys William Kunstler (1919–1995), Arthur Kinoy (1920–2003), Mortin Stavis (1915–1992), and Ben Smith (b. 1927). The organization saw itself as a vehicle for supporting the work of activists through the courts. The CCR chose cases to litigate not necessarily because the cases could be won but because litigation would raise the social awareness of the issue involved. Jules Lobel served as president of CCR.

13. A. Lynd and S. Lynd, *Stepping Stones*, 147.

14. Keith LaMar, interview by authors, 18 Sept. 2012, Ohio State Penitentiary, Youngstown, Ohio.

15. S. Lynd, *Accompanying*, 138.

16. See Barry Morley, "Beyond Consensus: Salvaging the Sense of the Meeting" (Pendle Hill Pamphlet Number 307; Wallingford, Pa.: Pendle Hill Publications, 1993), 1–96.

17. Keith LaMar, interviews by authors, 18 Sept. and 25 Oct. 2012, Ohio State Penitentiary, Youngstown, Ohio; Jason Robb, interviews by authors, 25 Sept. and 11 Nov. 2012, Ohio State Penitentiary, Youngstown, Ohio.

18. Keith LaMar, interviews by authors, 18 Sept. and 25 Oct. 2012, Ohio State Penitentiary, Youngstown, Ohio; Jason Robb, interviews by authors, 25 Sept. and 11 Nov. 2012, Ohio State Penitentiary, Youngstown, Ohio; see also S. Lynd, *Accompanying*, 132–33.

19. A. Lynd and S. Lynd, *Stepping Stones*, 154.

20. Ibid., 155–56.

11. Occupy and Accompany

1. Mark W. Weber, Notes on Intentional Communities Conference, 31 Aug.–3 Sept., 2012, Personal Notebook # 25, 4:786–94, 804.

2. Jennifer Baligush, "'Occupy' Movement Comes to Youngstown," WFMJ website, http://www.wfmj.com/story/15637641/occupy-movement-comes-to-youngstown.

3. The movement's slogan "We are the 99%" is most commonly thought to derive from a 2011 article by economist Joseph Stiglitz entitled "Of the 1%, by the 1%, for the 1%." In it, Stiglitz criticized an economy in which "the upper 1 percent of Americans are now taking in nearly a quarter of the nation's income every year," adding that "in terms of wealth rather than income, the top 1 percent control 40 percent" and claiming that these figures reflected an even more troubling "shrinking" of "equality of opportunity" (Joseph E.

Stiglitz, "Of the 1%, by the 1%, for the 1%," *Vanity Fair*, May 2011). After a Tumblr blogger known as Chris began a blog named "We are the 99%," in August 2011, the phrase became a movement catchword (see http://wearethe-99percent.tumblr.com/post/9289779051/we-are-the-99-percent).

4. S. Lynd, *Accompanying*, 153.

5. Ibid., 154.

6. Mark W. Weber, Notes on meeting with Alice and Staughton Lynd, 14 Jan. 2013, Personal Notebook #27, 5:247–55, 251.

7. Ibid.

12. The Lynds Today: An Assessment

1. Andrew Putz, "The Last Radical," *Cleveland Scene*, 23 May 2002. Electronic newsletter. http://www.clevescene.com/cleveland/the-last-radical/Content?oid=1479512.

2. Ibid.

3. Dan O'Brien, "For Staughton Lynd, the Fight Never Ends," *Business Journal* [Youngstown], 2 Mar. 1999; reproduced on weblog of Kenneth A. Rahn, Sr., http://www.kenrahn.com/JFK/The_critics/Lynd/Fight_never_ends.html.

4. Eric O'Neill and Lorry Swain, interview by authors, 23 Aug. 2013, northern Kentucky, near Portsmouth, Ohio.

5. Alexis Buss, telephone interview by authors, 11 Aug. 2013.

6. Howard Zinn, foreword to Mirra, *The Admirable Radical*, xv.

7. Jesse Lemisch, Staughton Lynd, and Robert Cohen, "Rebutting David Greenberg's Broadside on Howard Zinn," History News Network website, 19 May 2013, http://hnn.us/article/151106#sthash.G7cDHCV8.dpuf. See also David Greenberg, "Agit-Prof: Howard Zinn's Influential Mutilations of American History," *New Republic*, 25 Mar. 2013, reproduced on the *New Republic* website, http://www.newrepublic.com/article/112574/howard-zinns-influential-mutilations-american-history.

8. S. Lynd, "Howard Zinn, Historian" (paper presented at the 2010 conference of the Organization of American Historians, to a session called "Remembering Howard Zinn," hosted by the Labor and Working-Class History Association and Historians Against the War, 9 Apr. 2010, Washington, D.C.); reproduced on the Zinn Education Project website, http://zinnedproject.org/2010/04/howard-zinn-historian-by-staughton-lynd/.

9. Putz, "The Last Radical."

10. Ibid.

11. A. Lynd and S. Lynd, interview by authors, 18 Mar. 2010, Niles, Ohio.

12. Ibid.

13. A. Lynd and S. Lynd, interview by authors, 9 Sept. 2013, Niles, Ohio.

14. Gar Alperovitz, *What Then Must We Do? Straight Talk about the Next American Revolution* (White River Jct., Vt.: Chelsea Green, 2013), 33.

15. A. Lynd and S. Lynd, interview by authors, 18 Mar. 2010, Niles, Ohio.

16. Alperovitz, *What Then Must We Do?*, 30.

13. Final Words

1. Martha Lynd Altan, interview by authors, 14 July 2013, Niles, Ohio.

2. A. Lynd and S. Lynd, *Stepping Stones,* 179.

3. S. Lynd, *The Fight Against Shutdowns,* 42–44.

4. See S. Lynd, "The Individual Was Made for Community," *Liberation,* Jan. 1957, 15–18; and S. Lynd, "Can Men Live as Brothers? Lessons of a Nineteenth Century Community," *Liberation,* Feb. 1958, 12–14. A useful context for this perspective is provided by Dan McKanan in his book *Prophetic Encounters: Religion and the Radical Tradition* (Boston, Mass.: Beacon Press, 2011).

5. See S. Lynd, "The Individual Was Made for Community," 15–18; and S. Lynd, "Can Men Live as Brothers?" 12–14.

6. A. Lynd and S. Lynd, *Stepping Stones,* 179.

BIBLIOGRAPHY

Alperovitz, Gar. *America Beyond Capitalism: Reclaiming Our Wealth, Our Liberty, and Our Democracy.* Hoboken, N.J.: J. Wiley, 2005.

———. "Not So Wild a Dream." *The Nation,* 11 June 2002.

———, and Staughton Lynd. *Strategy and Program: Two Essays Toward A New American Socialism.* Boston: Beacon Press, 1973.

Avrich, Paul. "What is 'Makhaevism'?" *Soviet Studies* 17 (July 1965): 1:66. Reproduced at http://libcom.org/history/what-makhaevism-paul-avrich.

Badarcke, Frank. *Trampling Out the Vintage: Cesar Chavez and the Two Souls of the United Farmworkers.* London: Verso, 2011.

Benson, Herman. *Rebels, Reformers, and Racketeers: How Insurgents Transformed the Labor Movement.* Brooklyn, N.Y.: Association for Union Democracy, 2004.

Bossen, Colin. "The Chicago Couriers Union, 2003–2010: A Case Study in Solidarity Unionism." *Working USA: A Journal of Labor and Society* 15, no. 2 (June 2012): 197–215.

Branch, Taylor. *Pillar of Fire: America in the King Years, 1963–1965.* New York: Simon and Schuster, 1999.

Calverton, V. F., ed. *The Making of Society: An Outline of Sociology.* New York: Modern Library, 1937.

Coleman, Peter. *The Liberal Conspiracy: The Congress for Cultural Freedom and the Struggle for the Mind of Postwar Europe.* New York: Free Press, 1989.

Collier, Peter, and David Horowitz. *The Destructive Generation: Second Thoughts about the Sixties.* Glencoe, Ill.: Free Press, 1996.

Drier, Peter. "Rules for Radicals—and Conservatives: The Rightwing World Resurrects Saul Alinsky to Attack Obama." *Jewish Currents* 4, no. 4 (Summer 2012): 14–19.

Early, Steve. *Civil Wars in U.S. Labor: Birth of a New Workers' Movement or Death Throes of the Old?* Chicago: Haymarket Books, 2010.

———. *Embedded with Organized Labor: Journalistic Reflections on the Class War at Home.* New York: Monthly Review Press, 2009.

Fink, Leon. *Workingmen's Democracy: The Knights of Labor and American Politics.* Urbana: Univ. of Illinois Press, 1983.

Foot, John. "The Secret Life of Ignazio Silone." *New Left Review* 3 (May–June 2000): 146–52.

Fuechtmann, Thomas G. *Steeples and Stacks: Religion and the Steel Crisis in Youngstown.* Cambridge, Mass.: Cambridge Univ. Press, 1989.

Ganz, Marshall. *Why David Sometimes Wins.* New York: Oxford Univ. Press, 2009.

Gary Indiana Writers' Workshop and Staughton Lynd. *Two Steel Contracts.* Boston: New England Free Press, 1971. Pamphlet.

Genovese, Eugene D. "The Question." *Dissent,* Summer 1994, 371–76.

Getman, Julius. *Restoring Power of Unions: It Takes a Movement.* New Haven, Conn.: Yale Univ. Press, 2010.

Glaberman, Martin. *Punching Out and Other Writings.* Chicago: Charles H. Kerr Publishers, 2002.

Gross, Daniel, and Staughton Lynd. *Solidarity Unionism at Starbucks.* Oakland, Calif.: PM Press, 2011. Pamphlet.

Grubacic, Andrej, ed. *From Here to There: The Staughton Lynd Reader.* Oakland: PM Press, 2010.

Grzesiak, Michael P. "The Ecumenical Coalition of the Mahoning Valley: How Church Leaders Became Involved in the Steel Business." M.A. thesis, Department of Philanthropic Studies, Indiana University, May 2008.

Kelly, Daniel P. *James Burnham and the Struggle for the World: A Life.* Wilmington, Del.: ISI Books, 2002.

Leopold, Les. *The Man Who Hated Work and Loved Labor: The Life and Times of Tony Mazzocchi.* White River Junction, Vt.: Chelsea Green Press, 2007.

Lichtenstein, Nelson. *The Most Dangerous Man in Detroit: Walter Reuther and the Fate of American Labor.* New York: Basic Books, 1995.

Linkon, Sherry Lee, and John Russo. *Steeltown U.S.A.: Work and Memory in Youngstown.* Lawrence: Univ. of Kansas Press, 2002.

Lynd, Alice, and Staughton Lynd. *Rank and File: Personal Histories of Working-Class Organizers.* Boston: Beacon Press, 1973.

———. *Stepping Stones: A Memoir of a Life Together.* Lanham, Md.: Lexington Books, 2009.

Lynd, Staughton. *Accompanying: Pathways to Social Change.* Oakland, Calif.: PM Press, 2012.

———. *The Fight Against the Shutdowns: Youngstown's Steel Mill Closings.* San Pedro, Calif.: Singlejack Books, 1982.

———. "The Individual Was Made for Community." *Liberation* (Jan. 1957): 16–18.

———, ed. *Living Inside Our Hope: A Steadfast Radical's Thoughts on Rebuilding the Movement.* Ithaca, N.Y.: ILR Press, 1997.

———. "Oral History From Below." *Oral History Review* 21, no. 1 (Spring 1993): 1–8.

———. *Solidarity Unionism: Rebuilding the Labor Movement from the Bottom Up.* Chicago: Charles H. Kerr Publishing Co., 1992.

———. "Staughton Lynd, A Personal Letter." *Impact* 8, no. 1 (April 2000).

———, ed. *"We Are All Leaders": The Alternative Unionism of the 1930s.* Champaign, Ill.: Univ. of Illinois Press, 1966.

———. "Worker-Community Ownership in Youngstown?" *WIN Magazine,* 25 Jan. 1979.

———, and Alice Lynd. *New Rank and File.* Ithaca, N.Y.: ILR Press, 2000.

Lynd, Staughton, and Andrej Grubacic. *Wobblies and Zapatistas: Conversations on Anarchism, Marxism, and Radical History.* Oakland, Calif.: PM Press, 2008.

Lynd, Staughton, and Daniel Gross. *Labor Law for the Rank and Filer: Building Solidarity While Staying Clear of the Law*, 2d ed. Oakland, Calif.: PM Press, 2011.

Lynd, Staughton, Sam Bahour, and Alice Lynd, eds. *Homeland: Oral Histories of Palestine and Palestinians*. Ithaca, N.Y.: Olive Branch Press, 1994.

Lynd, Staughton, and Thomas Hayden. *The Other Side*. New York: New American Library, 1966.

McGee, James. "Union Health Care Plans Will Suffer Under Obamacare." *Labor Notes*, Mar. 2013, 14–15.

McKanan, Dan. *Prophetic Encounters: Religion and the Radical Tradition*. Boston, Mass.: Beacon Press, 2011.

Mills, C. Wright. *New Men of Power*. Champaign: Univ. of Illinois Press, 2001.

Mirra, Carl. *The Admirable Radical: Staughton Lynd and Cold War Dissent, 1945–1970*. Kent, Ohio: Kent State Univ. Press, 2010.

———. *Citizens and Soldiers: An Oral History of Operation Iraqi Freedom from the Battlefield to the Pentagon*. New York: Palgrave, 2008.

Montgomery, David. *The Fall of the House of Labor: The Workplace, The State, and American Labor Activism, 1865–1925*. Cambridge, Mass.: Cambridge Univ. Press, 1987.

Morley, Barry. "Beyond Consensus: Salvaging the Sense of the Meeting." Pendle Hill Pamphlet Number 307. Wallingford, Pa.: Pendle Hill Publications, 1993.

Morris, Charles J. *The Blue Eagle at Work: Reclaiming Democratic Rights in the American Workplace*. Ithaca, N.Y.: Cornell Univ. Press, 2005.

Newfield, Jack. *A Prophetic Minority*. New York: New American Library, 1966.

Nozick, Robert. *Anarchy, State, and Utopia*. New York: Basic Books, 1974.

Orser, Edward. *Searching for a Viable Alternative: The Macedonia Cooperative Community, 1937–1958*. New York: Lenox Hill Publishers, 1982.

Parker, Mike, and Martha Gruelle. *Democracy is Power: Rebuilding Unions from the Bottom Up*. Detroit, Mich.: Labor Notes, 1999.

Pawel, Miriam. *The Union of Their Dreams: Power, Hope, and Struggle in Cesar Chavez's Farm Worker Movement*. New York: Bloomsbury Press, 2009.

Petras, James. "The CIA and the Cold War Revisited." *Monthly Review* 51, no. 6 (Nov. 1999), 47–66. Review.

Rodgers, Daniel T. *The Age of Fracture*. Cambridge, Mass.: Belknap Press, 2011.

Sand, Shlomo. *The Invention of the Jewish People*. London: Verso, 2009.

———. *The Invention of the Land of Israel: From Holy Land to Homeland*. London: Verso, 2012.

Silone, Ignazio. *The Abruzzo Trilogy: Fontamara, Bread and Wine, and Seed Beneath the Snow*. Steerforth, Vt.: Steerforth Press, 2000.

Stern, Sol. "My Jewish Problem—and Ours: Israel, the Left, and the Jewish Establishment." *Ramparts*, Aug. 1971, 30–40.

Stillman, Don. *Stronger Together: The Story of SEIU*. White River Junction, Vt.: Chelsea Green, 2010.

Thompson, E. P., ed. *Out of Apathy*, London: Stevens, 1960.

Waters, Mary-Alice, ed. *Rosa Luxemburg Speaks*. New York: Pathfinder Press, 1970.

Weir, Robert. *Beyond Labor's Veil: The Culture of the Knights of Labor.* Philadelphia: Univ. of Pennsylvania Press, 1996.

———. *Knights Unhorsed: Internal Conflict in Gilded Age Social Movements.* Detroit, Mich.: Wayne State Univ. Press, 2000.

Williams, Gary, with Larry Dotson. *Siege in Lucasville: An Insider's Account and Critical Review of Ohio's Worst Prison Riot,* rev. ed. Bloomington, Ind.: Rooftop Publishers, 2006.

Winslow, Cal. *Labor's Civil War in California: The NUHW Healthcare Workers' Rebellion.* Oakland, Calif.: PM Press, 2010.

Wolcott, Roger. "The Church and Social Action: Steelworkers and Bishops in Youngstown." Paper presented at meeting of the Pennsylvania Sociological Society, Philadelphia, Pa., 3 Nov. 1979.

Worthman, Roy T. *From Syndicalism to Trade Unionism: The IWW in Ohio, 1905–1950.* New York: Garland Publishing Co., 1985.

Wreszin, Michael. *Rebel in Defense of Tradition: The Life and Politics of Dwight Macdonald.* New York: Basic Books, 1994.

Youngstown Committee of the Ohio Sesquicentennial Commission. *Industry and Commerce in Youngstown.* Youngstown, Ohio: N.p., 1953.

Zinn, Howard. *You Can't Stay Neutral on a Moving Train: A Personal History of Our Times.* Boston, Mass.: Beacon Press, 1994.

INDEX